MW01181762

THE BATTLE FOR TRUTH

Also by Glen O. Suiter

This is My Story: Growing in Grace

The Battle For Truth

How to Win the Spiritual War
With the Enemy of Your Soul

Glen O. Suiter

Published by:
Glen O. Suiter
Spokane, Washington

The Battle for Truth: How to Win the Spiritual War with the Enemy of Your Soul

Copyright 2020 Glen O. Suiter

All rights reserved. No part of this publication may be reproduced, stored in a retrieval system, or transmitted in any form or by any means, electronic, mechanical, photocopying, recording, scanning, or otherwise, except as permitted under Section 107 or 108 of the 1976 United States Copyright Act, without the prior written permission of the publisher.

Scripture quotations marked (ESV) are from The ESV® Bible (The Holy Bible, English Standard Version®), copyright © 2001 by Crossway, a publishing ministry of Good News Publishers. Used by permission. All rights reserved. Scripture quotations taken from the New American Standard Bible® (NASB), Copyright © 1960, 1962, 1963, 1968, 1971, 1972, 1973, 1975, 1977, 1995 by The Lockman Foundation Used by permission. www.Lockman.org. Scripture quotations marked (NLT) are taken from the Holy Bible, New Living Translation, copyright ©1996, 2004, 2015 by Tyndale House Foundation. Used by permission of Tyndale House Publishers, a Division of Tyndale House Ministries, Carol Stream, Illinois 60188. All rights reserved. Scripture quotations marked (NIV) are taken from the Holy Bible, New International Version®, NIV®. Copyright © 1973, 1978, 1984, 2011 by Biblica, Inc.™ Used by permission of Zondervan. All rights reserved worldwide. www.zondervan.com The "NIV" and "New International Version" are trademarks registered in the United States Patent and Trademark Office by Biblica, Inc.™
All scripture is from the King James Version unless otherwise noted.

For more information or to contact the author, Glen O. Suiter:
Email: glenosuiter@hotmail.com

Book and cover design: Russel Davis www.graydogpress.com
Book editor: Barbara Hollace www.barbarahollace.com

ISBN: 978-1-7345159-0-9

Printed in the United States of America

Acknowledgements

It is with great appreciation that I recognize the following people as contributors to *The Battle for Truth*. Each one has encouraged me in writing this book and supported me in this endeavor.

Pastor Eldon Rayborn, Norma Jackson, and Ron Hand who reviewed the manuscript, giving me constructive feedback.

Barbara Hollace who worked with me as a writing coach, editor, and so much more.

My wife, Donna, for the endless hours she put into checking and rechecking to make sure the manuscript was ready for publishing.

Russ Davis of Gray Dog Press for his professional help in publishing the book.

Contents

Introduction

Our world is the battleground for the spiritual war raging between Satan, the god of this world and Jehovah, the Creator of heaven and earth. Although our battle is against an unseen enemy, the effects are very real and visible.

Today there seems to be more confusion, trouble, anxiety, frustration, fear, and hopelessness than in the days of my youth. Even within the Christian community there seems to be a lack of confidence as Satan seeks to disrupt our peace, confidence, and trust in the living God of the Bible. We seem to forget that Satan is a defeated foe. Have we deliberately closed our minds to the enemy's tactics or are we blinded by his deception? Our quest is to turn away from our frustration and find peace.

As Christians, the question comes, how are we to live in a world controlled by Satan? The Bible says, *My people are destroyed for lack of knowledge* (Hosea 4:6). *The Battle for Truth* was written, so that as Christians, we will be better informed about the enemy we face and how to live a life of victory. My prayer is that together we will be stirred up in our minds and encouraged in our hearts to daily fight this spiritual battle. We do not face the enemy alone. The living God of the Bible is fighting with us and for us. Victory belongs to the Lord!

Together in His Service,

Glen O. Suiter

1
The War Zone

Several years ago, I was introduced to a program called *Your Wish Is Your Command*. It was based on the Law of Attraction. Whatever you desire, focus your attention on it, and the universe will bring it to you. This was a motivational program designed to help anyone achieve their heart's desire, be it financial, or excel in any desired activity. The program sounded good to me, and for a while, I thought it was a good program. However, the more I looked into the program, the more I became aware that it was a New Age concept to replace Christian biblical teaching.

As a result, I became interested in the subject of spiritual warfare, add to that some situations occurred causing me to be concerned with the acceptance of New Age teaching. More than a hundred million Americans claim no allegiance to a church, synagogue, or temple, but they are looking for meaning in their lives. They are seeking some higher supremacy that will fill their inner emptiness. Also, they are told that they can do this without believing church doctrines, without acknowledging their sins, and without having to commit to the Creator of the universe. Their cry is, yes, I want to have a connection to the spiritual, but I want to do it on my terms; terms that honor who I am as a discerning, thoughtful person.

We are inundated with a host of New Age teachers, Eastern religions, and self-proclaimed spiritual guides all seeking to aid man in his search. Many celebrities, talk show hosts, internet gurus, and books all attempt to lead people into a spiritual experience without the need to trust in the living God of the Bible.

However, one must subscribe to their teaching with full devotion to receive the benefit espoused. If one can obtain the full advantage without a change of heart, there is no need to surrender to God.

This battle is an eternal battle with the outcome being eternity with Christ in heaven, or with Satan, the god of this world in hell. The battle rages between the living God, the Creator of heaven and earth, (Isaiah 43:10, 44:6, 46:9) and what the Bible calls "the god of this world" (John 12:31, 14:30, 16:11; 2 Corinthians 4:4; Ephesians 2:2). The enemy we are facing is not flesh and blood, but a spiritual enemy. Our enemy has a name commonly known as Satan or Devil. Satan's greatest tool is deception. If you will believe his lies and buy into a false concept of God and the Bible, the Devil has accomplished his desired goal, of successfully redirecting your worship from God to himself. Whoever does not worship God, worships Satan.

Deception in the name of tolerance and reason seems to be the marketing tool of the day. Men are chasing after everything that sounds good and is pleasant to their thinking, with no thought of where they will end up. The irony of all this is that the church is not exempt from buying into these deceptions in the name of being tolerant and reasonable. Dave Reagan of *Lamb and Lion Ministries* points out that only 9% of Americans are Bible-believing Christians. Even more shocking, only 17% of professing Christians are truly Bible-believing Christians, which explains the situation where we find ourselves.

As Christians, it is of utmost importance that we stand firm on what the Bible says. Jesus gave a solemn warning, "Be not deceived." He was so emphatic concerning deception that Jesus mentioned it three times in His discourse of the end times in Matthew the 24th chapter.

> *And Jesus answered and said unto them, Take heed that no man deceive you. For many shall come in my name, saying, I am Christ; and shall deceive many* (Matthew 24:4-5).

> *And many false prophets shall rise, and shall deceive many* (Matthew 24:11).

For there shall arise false Christs, and false prophets, and shall shew great signs and wonders; insomuch that, if it were possible, they shall deceive the very elect (Matthew 24:24).

I have always thought that there would be men who claimed to be Christ who would draw a following to them. Such was the case a few years ago with Father Devine, who claimed to be the Messiah. Jim Jones and David Koresh deceived many. Today there are those who say they are speaking for God, and others relate how Jesus has appeared and given them messages. I don't see any difference between a person claiming to be the Messiah, speaking for Jesus, or someone saying He is in the desert or the secret chamber. In each situation, they fall under the warning Jesus gave in Matthew 24:4,5,11,24,26.

I have read some of the writings that were supposedly the words of Jesus to this world. The message they espouse and the message of the Bible are not the same. There is no mention of the need to be born again (John 3:3). There is no mention of reconciliation by way of the cross (Colossians 1:20-22). No mention of the Blood for the atonement of sin (Colossians 1:20). We find no mention of Christ's priesthood (Hebrews 3:1, 4:15-16). No mention of the return of Christ (John 14:1-3; Acts 1:11). There is no mention of a Judgment Day or hell as a place of eternal torment and separation from God (Matthew 10:28).

I am left to wonder if this is Jesus speaking to us today, why is the message different? The Bible says that Satan's biggest and best tool in his arsenal is deception and lies. The Bible says, *For such are false apostles, deceitful workers, transforming themselves into the apostles of Christ. And no marvel; for Satan himself is transformed into an angel of light. Therefore it is no great thing if his ministers also be transformed as the ministers of righteousness; whose end shall be according to their works* (2 Corinthians 11:13-15).

Satan, as a deceiver, promises things that he will not or cannot deliver. He promises Godhood but not equal to Jehovah because

Jehovah is omnipotent (all-powerful), omniscient (all-knowing), and omnipresent (present everywhere), like the air we breathe. Satan promises that we will be like God in running our own lives and in charge of our destiny. The teachers who teach mind expansion, the Law of Attraction, universal law, and that we are gods or goddesses promise those who follow their teaching will receive great rewards. Some who subscribe to the teaching wholeheartedly, and commit to their program do produce excellent results; thus, drawing more people into the net of deception. The sad part is the majority end up with a feeling of despair and back in their old routine of just existing from day-to-day.

Where are we going as a church and a nation? This is my concern. These programs, events, and the deception they sow are why I have written this book. My goal is to show you that we are in a spiritual war with the enemy of our soul, with eternity the outcome. The question remains, to whom are we going to listen? My hope is that this writing will give a clear picture of the enemy and that he will be exposed for what he is. We do not need to be defeated or give in to his attacks. We can live a life of victory, peace, and security in Christ.

2
We Have An Enemy

Dr. David Jeremiah in his series of messages, *I Never Thought I Would See The Day*, stated I never thought I would see the day when Christians wouldn't know they were in a war. The Christian's spiritual enemy is not in uniform, and he doesn't meet us on an identifiable battlefield. He uses ruthless unconventional tactics, such as deceit, deflection, and disguise.

It is incredible to me that so little is known about this enemy. Being raised in the church, we were taught that there was a devil whose name was Satan, and he went around like a roaring lion. We were also taught, or it was implied, not to give Satan much thought, or not to think of him at all. Just don't give Satan any place, and he will leave you alone. While the idea seems good, it doesn't hold much water. The scripture teaches that we have an enemy called Satan, or the Devil, and that enemy is continually on a mission to disrupt, hinder, deceive, and destroy us.

The Bible says, *My people are destroyed for lack of knowledge* (Hosea 4:6). Reading the struggles that Israel had with idolatry, the battles they fought with their enemies and the destruction of Israel and Judah by Nebuchadnezzar all because they turned away from God to serve idols, it would seem good to know something about this enemy. Jesus said, *The thief comes not, but for to steal, and to kill, and to destroy* (John 10:10). The more we know and understand that we are in a war with the archenemy of our soul, the better we can counter his attacks and live a victorious life.

Dietrich Bonhoeffer in speaking of the enemy of our soul says:

> "They (man) need a power stronger than that of the
> Prince of this world, the Devil... Although it is his
> cleverest trick to deny his power and to pretend that

he does not exist. It is just the supreme cunning of his that must be countered: he must be brought to light, and overcome through the power of the Christ."[1]

As I began to think about this, I started to search the scripture where the "Devil" is mentioned and discovered the Bible has quite a bit to say on this subject. The word "devil" is not in the Old Testament, but it appears that the word "the Devil" and "Satan" are used interchangeably to describe the same personage. The name "Satan" is used 19 times in the Old Testament and 36 times in the New Testament for a combination of 55 times in the Bible. The word "Devil" is used 61 times in 57 sections in the New Testament. The term "devils" is used four times in four sections in the Old Testament, and 51 times in 44 sections in the New Testament.

The term "devils" appears in Leviticus and Deuteronomy. These refer to sacrificing to devils in idolatrous worship. Psalm 106:37 says, *Yea, they sacrificed their sons and their daughters unto devils.* Leviticus 17:7 says, *They shall no more offer their sacrifices unto devils, after whom they have gone a whoring.* According to scripture, it appears that devils were a prominent figure in the Old Testament. Whether using the term "the Devil" or "devils", it is evident that the personage is the same, the enemy of our soul.

It isn't my desire to give any place or glory to the enemy but to equip us with the tools needed to effectively know when we are under attack, and how to defend ourselves. As Christians the battle is already won, the enemy is defeated. However, we are still under attack because we are living in the enemy's world. The Bible says that Satan is the god of this world. I will expand on this later. The more we know, the better we are able to deflect his attacks and live victoriously.

Rabbi Avi Lipkip of Jerusalem commented that Satan desires to kill or destroy all people because they are created in the image of God. As we look at the effects of sin in our world today, it is evident that the enemy is determined to destroy, deface, counterfeit, and weaken everything that God made, and called good. We are faced every day with the decision to surrender or resist the lust of the flesh, the lust of the eye, or the pride of life. Our sexuality is turned upside down; our marriages are broken; human life has been devalued; evil has been called good and good, evil. David Kupelian in his book, *The Marketing of Evil,* points out how far we have fallen as a nation when we embrace evil and reject biblical morality.

Who is this enemy of whom we know so little? How does this enemy work to make our lives ineffective? It appears that we must deal with a host of unseen enemies. Paul tells us, *For we wrestle not against flesh and blood, but against principalities, against powers, against the rulers of the darkness of this world, against spiritual wickedness in high places* (Ephesians 6:12). If we are contending with unseen enemies, it would be helpful to know something about them.

As Christians, we are not of this world, but we are in this world. We are in the territory of our enemy – the god of this world. When Jesus prayed that last night before His crucifixion, He made it clear that believers are not of this world. John 17:16 says, *They are not of the world even as I am not of the world,* and in John 17:15 (ESV), Jesus prayed, *I do not ask that you take them out of the world, but that you keep them from the evil one.* It is in this darkened world that we are to let our light shine and doing that will bring attacks from our enemy. He will use every trick imaginable to extinguish our light, or at least dim it to render us ineffective.

When we receive Christ and are born again, we are no longer citizens of this world. Our citizenship is transferred from earth to heaven. Paul said, *For our citizenship is in heaven,* (Philippians 3:20 NASB). Jesus said in His discussion with Nicodemus, that which is born of the flesh is flesh (earthly), and that which is born of spirit is spirit (heavenly). Signifying that as a child of God, we are not of this world; we, therefore, are in conflict with the god of this world. William Gurnall in his book, *The Christian in Complete Armor* writes:

"If God is with me, why is all this befallen me? ... The
state of grace is the commencing of a war against sin,
not the ending of it. ... There are two nations within
thee, two contrary nations, one from earth, earthly,
and the other from heaven, heavenly."[2]

We are at war with the unseen world and, unless we become
aware of where the battle is waged, we will be in a continual state
of anxiety and confusion. The Bible says, *God is not the author of
confusion, but of peace* (1 Corinthians 14:33). For a person to live
a life of victory, it is necessary for us to know our enemy. We also
need to know how to respond when under attack.

3
Our Enemy

For we wrestle not against flesh and blood, but
against principalities, against powers, against the
rulers of the darkness of this world, against spiritual
wickedness in high places.
Ephesians 6:12

This spiritual enemy is not in uniform, and he doesn't meet us on an identifiable battlefield. He shows up in church, in our homes, the workplace, at school, and any place where people come together for worship, business, education, or relaxation. He attacks his subjects at their weakest or their least expected moment with the *lust of the flesh, the lust of the eye, and the pride of life* (1 John 2:16). What are the lust of the flesh, the lust of the eye, and the pride of life?

Lust
Lust is a psychological force producing intense wanting for an object, or circumstance fulfilling the emotion. Lust can take any form, such as the lust for sexuality, money, or power.

The Lust of the Flesh
Anything that appeals to the desire of the senses, what gives me pleasure, whatever meets my needs. Not all pleasure is wrong, not all needs are wrong, what makes them lustful is when they take control of us, and we compromise our morality to satisfy them. Sensuality is the added attraction to lust; it is that which gives pleasure to the senses.

The Lust of the Eye

When we see things that we must have regardless of who it hurts, or what it takes to get it for our pleasure or prestige. The Bible calls this covetousness; the world calls this greed.

The Pride of Life

The lust for power for whatever I can accomplish, look at me see what I have built. Pride could also be self-protection; I will take care of myself and mine. Rather than trusting in the Lord for our provision, the Bible says, *But seek ye first the kingdom of God, and His righteousness; and all of these things shall be added unto you* (Matthew 6:33). That doesn't mean that we sit down and wait for things to appear, but to place our trust in God for everything every day. Pride is the attitude Satan displayed in Isaiah 14:12-14.

Paul sees this enemy as an unseen power behind the physical, mental, emotional, and relational struggles that we face, *For we wrestle not against flesh and blood* (Ephesians 6:12). As Christians, we may not be tempted to what we call "out and out sin", but we are faced with many attacks, identified as temptations. Attacks regarding our faith, such as patience, anger, despair, gossiping, the list is endless. This enemy while unseen, the effects of his attacks are very real. If we are not on guard, we will fall prey to those attacks. Our enemy *walks around like a roaring lion seeking whom he may devour* (1 Peter 5:8). He is also the god of this world and as such is a liar, a thief, a murderer, an accuser, and the power behind governments.

What does the Bible say about our enemy and his character, what makes him what he is? How can we know when we are under attack from the enemy? Look at the scripture and see what it says about each of his attributes: a roaring lion, a liar, thief, murderer, an accuser, and the power behind governments.

A Roaring Lion

Be sober, be vigilant; because of your adversary the devil, as a roaring lion, walketh about, seeking whom he may devour (1 Peter 5:8).

Stay alert! Watch out for your great enemy, the devil. He prowls around like a roaring lion, looking for someone to devour (1 Peter 5:8 NLT).

What comes to mind when we think of a roaring lion? I have always thought that a lion was like a wild beast in the jungle. That if we kept our eyes open, we would see him and know that he was there and we could avoid him. I was always looking for the lion in its physical body. Sounds good, but as I think on this scripture, it speaks to the character of the lion as frightening, intimidating, and cunning.

The events of the past few years have brought to mind how the Devil acts like a roaring lion. If you disagree with the Devil's crowd, you are yelled at, cursed, called all kinds of obscene names, and made to feel like you are the most unkind person in the world. The whole idea is to make you crawl back into your hole and not speak out against the sins that we are facing. Our world is turned upside down, and what was called good is now called evil, and what was called evil is now called good. If you stand for biblical morality, you are a hater. Never mind that the ones calling you a hater hate you and the things you stand for. To me, that is what the roaring lion is all about.

Another characteristic of the lion is his cunning ability to hide and wait for his prey. Not unlike our enemy who sneaks in unnoticed and then pounces on his subject unexpectedly. I see this as the enemy sneaking into the church in small increments, little steps. First, change some of the old established concepts of worship; bring worship up to modern standards. Don't be too strict as to morals; we won't talk about lifestyles. Soon we become so much like the world that you can't tell the difference. I have spoken with some who say, "I don't want to hear anything about hell and judgments because it makes me feel uncomfortable." I have talked with others who say they don't want to talk to their children about spiritual things. They want them to decide on their own when they are old enough – thus giving the enemy ample time to indoctrinate them with his teaching. My, how we have fallen into the trap of the lion!

A Liar

When he speaketh a lie, he speaketh of his own: for he is a liar and the father of it (John 8:44).

When he lies, it is consistent with his character; for he is a liar and the father of lies (John 8:44 NLT).

If someone claims, "I know God," but doesn't obey God's commandments, that person is a liar and is not living in the truth (1 John 2:4 NLT).

It is easy to think of Satan as a liar because we are acquainted with his lies recorded in scripture. We see how Satan manipulates scripture to accomplish deceit, like when he was talking with Eve, and when he tempted Christ. What we are less likely to see is when he is encouraging us to lie. We think that is just us trying to cover up a bad situation or not wanting to offend someone. That could be, but it could be that the Devil is endeavoring to trap us into a habit. And, when we see a nation that is being manipulated and controlled by liars, what are we to think? Does the father of liars inspire them? Is that why lying is so prevalent today?

A Thief

The thief cometh not, but for to steal, and to kill, and to destroy (John 10:10).

The thief's purpose is to steal and kill and destroy (John 10:10 NLT).

As we think about this, the question comes, what is the thief stealing from us? After all, we are in the camp of our Creator, right? Think about it, how many times has our peace been stolen because of a misunderstanding? Our joy, because of misplaced expectations? When we are going through a desert in life, the enemy is there to steal our trust in God.

A Murderer
> *He was a murderer from the beginning, and abode not in the truth, because there is no truth in him* (John 8:44).

> *For you are the children of your father, the devil, and you love to do the evil things he does. He was a murderer from the beginning. He has always hated the truth because there is no truth in him* (John 8:44 NLT).

> *Whosoever hateth his brother is a murderer: and ye know that no murderer hath eternal life abiding in him* (1 John 3:15).

When we think of Satan as a murderer, we know that he was behind Cain when he killed his brother. We know that he was involved in the effort to kill Joseph. We read how Satan, through Saul, tried to kill David. We think that was only in the Bible days and dismiss the fact that he is alive and working today to kill or destroy everything that God created.

Satan duped the children of Israel into sacrificing their sons and daughters unto devils (Psalm 106:36-38). Are we, as a nation, any different today? Since 1973, we have been offering our unborn children on the altar. Just recently the government has advocated making it lawful to kill a living child – we will keep the child comfortable until a decision is made, and they call it abortion.

Jesus said, *The thief comes only to steal and kill and destroy* (John 10:10 ESV). All murders are driven by Satan. He is motivated by his hatred for God and is out to destroy anything God created and called good. Any physical destruction is murder. When people are trapped by destructive addiction, when the home is ripped apart, when hope is lost, life becomes meaningless. This may be a slow death, but it is murder by Satan.

Satan has spread the lie that life has no value. Therefore, suicide is an epidemic. Abortion is an easy way out. School shootings and mass killings are the results. He murders by saying, *You shall not surely die.* There is no afterlife to be concerned about the consequences. A quick fix is to commit suicide, and it will all be over. The truth is, there is a day of judgment; it determines whether you will spend eternity in heaven with God or in hell with Satan.

An Accuser

For the accuser of our brethren is cast down, which accused them before our God day and night (Revelation 12:10).

For the accuser of our brothers and sisters has been thrown down to earth – the one who accuses them before our God day and night. And they have defeated him by the blood of the Lamb and by their testimony (Revelation 12:10-11 NLT).

Who of us has not lived with past regrets? Open sin, a secret sin, bad choices, dumb things that we would love to forget. We asked God to forgive us and to cleanse us from all iniquities, and we have been washed clean by the blood of Christ. Those things come up at the most inappropriate time. We struggle with the past asking God over and over again to forgive us. This is an example of the enemy coming as an accuser. It is his work to keep us upset and defeat us so that our light will not shine. If we are living in the past, we are not living in victory.

There are several ways that we can defeat the enemy when attacked by things of the past. We can remind the enemy that those sins are under the blood and that it is no longer an issue.

One method I have used when troubled by the past is to quote Philippians 3:13, *Forgetting those things that are behind, and reaching forth unto those things which are before.* Whatever method you choose to use to defeat the accuser, know that God is on your side and He is there to bring you victory over the past.

The Power Behind Governments

We are more familiar with the personal attacks such as liar, thief, murderer, and accuser, but not as familiar with his working in the governments of the world. We struggle with the direction our nation is going. We ask ourselves, what in the world is going on? Our world is turned upside down; there seems to be so much hatred. It seems that the ones calling for love are the very ones who hate unless you agree with them. Could there be a power behind what is happening that is beyond flesh and blood? As we look at how Satan was involved in the governments of Bible times, perhaps this will give us a better understanding of the conflict that our society is engaged in, and confirm that the Devil is the god of this world.

In the book of Isaiah, the prophet is speaking against the king of Babylon, then shifts from talking about the king to the power behind the king. The prophet describes Satan's fall from heaven and the reason for his fall. From this passage, we learn our enemy's name, the reason for his fall, and that he weakens the nations.

> *How art thou fallen from heaven, <u>O Lucifer</u>, son of the morning! How art thou cut down to the ground, which didst <u>weaken the nations</u>! For thou hast said in thine heart, <u>I will ascend </u>into heaven, <u>I will exalt</u> my throne above the stars of God: <u>I will sit </u>also upon the mount of the congregation, in the sides of the north: <u>I will ascend</u> above the heights of the clouds; <u>I will be like the most High</u>* (Isaiah 14:12-14).

We learn that his name is Lucifer; that pride was his downfall. Notice how many times the words "I will" are found in his statement. Self-exaltation is the pride that separates many from God. "I will do things my way; I don't need to answer to God." It reminds me of the song by Frank Sinatra, *I Did it My Way*.

The prophet Ezekiel is speaking against the king of Tyrus in the twenty-eighth chapter, and the eleventh verse shifts from the king to the power behind the king. Listen to how Ezekiel describes this personage.

> *Moreover the word of the LORD came unto me, saying, Son of man, take up a lamentation upon the king of Tyrus, and say unto him, Thus saith the Lord God; Thou sealest up the sum, full of wisdom, and perfect in beauty. Thou hast been in Eden the garden of God; every precious stone was thy covering, the sardius, topaz, and the diamond, the beryl, the onyx, and the jasper, the sapphire, the emerald, and the carbuncle, and gold: the workmanship of thy tabrets and of thy pipes was prepared in thee in the day that thou wast created. Thou art the anointed cherub that covereth; and I have set thee so: thou wast upon the holy mountain of God; thou hast walked up and down in the midst of the stones of fire. Thou wast perfect in thy ways from the day that thou wast created, till iniquity was found in thee* (Ezekiel 28:11-15).

Lest we think that Satan is not the ruler of this world and the power behind governments, remember when Jesus was tempted in the wilderness by the Devil. One of the three temptations was when Satan took Jesus up onto a very high mountain and showed him all of the kingdoms of the world. And said, *I will give you all of the kingdoms of the world if you will fall down and worship me* (Matthew 4:8-9). Jesus never questions his ownership or authority over the kingdoms, therefore confirming that they were his to give. With Satan as the god of this world, it is his power behind the ungodly powers that seeks control of governments.

Daniel gives us a clear picture of the unseen battle that is taking place in the heavens. While Daniel was praying, an angel appeared to him and explained that from the first day of his prayer, God heard his request. The angel told Daniel that he was dispatched with the message from God that very day. The angel then explained that while on his way, he was stopped by the Prince of Persia and was unable to continue until Michael came to assist him. What we see is a picture of the unseen battles that take place in the heavens. The angel said that because of Michael's help, he was able to deliver God's message to Daniel. The angel then explains that he must return to fight with the Prince of Persia and that the Prince of Grecia shall come.

> *Then said he unto me, Fear not, Daniel: for from the first day that thou didst set thine heart to understand, and to chasten thyself before thy God, thy words were heard, and I am come for thy words. But the <u>prince of the kingdom of Persia withstood me one and twenty days</u>: but, lo, <u>Michael, one of the chief princes, came to help me;</u> and I remained there with the kings of Persia* (Daniel 10:12-13).

> *And now will I return to fight with the <u>prince of Persia</u>: and when I am gone forth, lo, the <u>prince of Grecia</u> shall come* (Daniel 10:20).

Job also gives us a glimpse of the unseen conflict between God and Satan with mankind as the trophy (Job 1:7-22). Paul identifies the enemy as the god of this world, the one who blinds people's minds, so they are unable to see the truth of God and His Word.

> *In whom <u>the god of this world hath blinded the minds of them which believe not,</u> lest the light of the glorious gospel of Christ, who is the image of God, should shine unto them* (2 Corinthians 4:4).

Jesus identifies our enemy as the prince of this world.

> *Hereafter I will not talk much with you: for the <u>prince of this world cometh, and hath nothing in me</u>* (John 14:30).

The Pharisees acknowledged the ranking of devils when they said that Jesus was casting out demons by the prince of devils.

> *But the Pharisees said, He casteth out devils through the prince of the devils* (Matthew 9:34).

> *This fellow doth not cast out devils, but by Beelzebub the prince of the devils* (Matthew 12:24).

> *And the scribes which came down from Jerusalem said, He hath Beelzebub, and by the prince of the devils casteth he out devils* (Mark 3:22).

William Gurnall, in his book, *The Christian in Complete Armour,* says, "Jeroboam is said to ordain priests for devils, 2 Chronicles 11:15; and therefore he [Satan] is called not only the prince but the god of this world because he hath the worship of a god-given him."[3]

We have an enemy that is always on the move looking for a weakness in our armor. When he finds a place to sling his darts, he comes with such force, suddenness, and subtlety, we are taken entirely by surprise. Caught unaware, we either surrender to the temptation or fight. It is times like this that we need to step back and evaluate the situation and ask, is this an attack or a bump in the road?

We come under attack at our most vulnerable times. When we are suffering emotionally, or are physically worn out, when under stress of any kind, these are the times when Satan attacks. The enemy comes and suggests that our needs are not being fulfilled; therefore we should take advantage of the opportunity that is before us, be it sexual, financial, emotional, or any number of temptations that we encounter. It is at this time we need to realize that our battle is not with flesh and blood, but with the prince and power of this world. We must learn that our struggle is an unseen battle that appears to be with flesh and blood, but in reality, it is with the god of this world. William Gurnall put it this way:

> "The stress of the saint's battle; not in resisting flesh and blood, but principalities and powers. ... for the war is against the serpent and his seed; as wide as the world is, it cannot peaceably hold the saints and wicked together."[4]

From the scripture, we learn that we have an unseen enemy who is the god of this world. This enemy hates God and anyone that identifies with God. Jesus said for us not to be disturbed when we are attacked by the enemy because, if he hated Him, he would hate us. This enemy though unseen, used his visible subjects to wreak havoc on Job, causing him much suffering, pain, and loss. This enemy is ever watchful seeking the opportunity to take us down with sin, despair, and/or discouragement.

The apostle John points out that, All that is in the world, *the lust of the flesh, and the lust of the eyes, and the pride of life, is not of the Father, but is of the world* (1 John 2:16). That is what drives the world. As a child of God, our nature has been changed from that of the world to Christ-likeness. However, as long as we are in this body, we are subject to the attacks of the enemy: the lust of the flesh, the lust of the eyes, and the pride of life. Our enemy watches for our weak moments to tempt us with the desires of the flesh. It is therefore imperative that we know who our enemy is, and how to recognize when we are under attack.

John said, *Love not the world, neither the things that are in the world. If any man loves the world, the love of the Father is not in him. For all that is in the world, the lust of the flesh, and the lust of the eyes, and the pride of life, is not of the Father, but is of the world. And the world passeth away, and the lust thereof: but he that doeth the will of God abideth for ever* (1 John 2:15-17). The closer we get to the Father, the less we are drawn away by the lust of the flesh. If we are struggling with things of the world, and our desires are more for this world than God, we need to reexamine our commitment. God brings total victory when we surrender to Him and cling to the Word – the Bible.

Sometimes we are just derailed by a bump in the road of life. Not every negative thing that happens in life is an attack from Satan. Jesus said in Matthew 5:45, *for he maketh his sun to rise on the evil and on the good, and sendeth rain on the just and on the unjust.* Natural events such as storms, fires, earthquakes, sickness, war, and politics affect all of us. These things happen just because we are living in a broken world, and may not be an attack from Satan. Nevertheless, we should be vigilant to weigh everything to see if we are under attack, then respond accordingly. When we respond correctly to trials and temptations, we grow in the Lord. James tells us, *Consider it a great joy, my brothers, whenever you experience various trials, knowing that the testing of your faith produces endurance. But endurance must do its complete work, so that you may be mature and complete, lacking nothing* (James 1:2-4 HCSB).

Let us, therefore, hold fast to the Lord and in the power of His might to stand firm in a world where we are just pilgrims and strangers.

4
Our Armor

Finally, my brethren, be strong in the Lord, and the power
of his might. Put on the whole armor of God, that ye may be
able to stand against the wiles of the devil. For we wrestle not
against flesh and blood, but against principalities, against
powers, against the rulers of the darkness of this world, against
spiritual wickedness in high places. Wherefore take unto you
the whole armor of God, that ye may be able to withstand in
the evil day, and having done all, to stand. Stand therefore,
having your loins girt about with truth, and having on the
breastplate of righteousness; And your feet shod with the
preparation of the gospel of peace; Above all, taking the shield
of faith, wherewith ye shall be able to quench all the fiery
darts of the wicked. And take the helmet of salvation, and the
sword of the Spirit, which is the word of God: Praying always
with all prayer and supplication in the Spirit, and watching
thereunto with all perseverance and supplication for all saints.
Ephesians 6:10-18

Why Do We Need God's Armor?

Satan comes as a serpent, in the person of false teachers, and through them labors to deceive us with lies. Satan comes like a lion, causing us to fear reprisals or bodily harm. Satan comes as an accuser, reminding us of all our failures and shortcomings. The more we understand how the enemy attacks, the more we can stand against him. We are being attacked from every direction by what we hear, by what we see, by what we read, and by thoughts placed in our minds by an enemy bent on making our lives difficult, and to deceive us.

Paul begins this section by saying, *For we wrestle not against flesh and blood, but against principalities, against powers, against the rulers of the darkness of this world, against spiritual wickedness in high places* (Ephesians 6:12). He then tells us to stand firm, *and having done all to stand.*

STAND. This statement has troubled me, because if we have exhausted all of our strength to stand, how are we able to continue to stand? As I thought on this, the scripture came to mind of the predicament the children of Israel found themselves in at the Red Sea.

Following the Passover, they were led by God out of Egypt by way of the Red Sea. There they found themselves boxed in unable to move forward and Pharaoh's army coming up behind them. It looked as if God had led them to an impasse; they were trapped, the sea before them, and the enemy behind them. From their perspective, God had led them to their death and destruction. To add insult to injury, the wind begins to blow. As if life wasn't bad enough, they were trapped with nowhere to go, and now the weather turns against them. Little did they know that God was in the process of bringing them deliverance, and at the same time, destruction to their enemy. Amid their fear and frustration, Moses spoke the word of the Lord, *Fear ye not, stand still, and see the salvation of the Lord* (Exodus 14:13).

How many times have we found ourselves in such a situation? Having surrendered our life to God, we are committed to following Him no matter what, and then find ourselves in a situation beyond our ability to handle it. What are we to do? We are to follow the same pattern that God gave Israel and the words that Paul gave us, having done all to stand, "Stand." Stand still and see the salvation of the Lord. God has a plan to deliver us and defeat the enemy at the same time.

It is amazing, as I reflect on life, how many times when faced with a situation where we feel boxed in that we begin searching for a way out that will satisfy us and save face at the same time. We seek counsel from friends and family. Looking this way and that way, we seek a solution to our predicament. That is the time we need to stand still and seek God for His answer. Waiting is not one of our strongest character qualities. We want the answer now, and to our satisfaction, never mind what God's plan may be.

How many times when we feel we have been wronged, or our expectations not met, we set out to make things right according to our thinking? We don't even give God a chance to work on our behalf.

I have known people who were experts at manipulating things to satisfy their own desire and provide them with the feeling that this was God's will. It, therefore, looked to them that it was God's will for them to have, do, or experience the things they thought would bring about the best results to fulfill their desires. They were always things that brought immediate satisfaction to their way of thinking. Many times their actions undermined the will of God, and the results were costly to them and others. A biblical example is when Abraham and Sarah took matters into their own hands, and Ishmael was born. We are still living with the consequences of that decision.

5

Girdle of Truth

. . . having your loins girt about with truth . . .

The first article is the girdle of truth. The attack on truth is one of the areas that Satan is making huge inroads today. We are being bombarded every day by attacks on the truth. How do we know what the truth is? False teachers are teaching that the Word of God is no longer relevant today. We are told that what is true for you might not be true for me. Everyone has their truth; this widespread belief is called relativism. The New Age movement and Eastern religions have their gurus that teach that the old ways of relating to God are antiquated and no longer apply.

Ravi Zacharias says in his book, *Why Jesus?*:

> "The greatest and most notable casualty of our times in which we are inundated with spiritual terminology is, unquestionably, truth. … From the news to the weather to advertising to entertainment, we are sold feelings, not truth."[5]

Dietrich Bonhoeffer writes in his book, *The Cost of Discipleship*:

> "Both modern theology and secular totalitarianism hold pretty much in common that the message of the Bible has to be adapted, more or less, to the requirements of a secular world. No wonder, therefore, that the process of debasing Christianity as inaugurated by liberal theology led in the long run, to a complete perversion and falsification of the essence of Christian teaching by National Socialism."[6]

Ravi Zacharias also points out in his book, *Why Jesus?*, many false teachers are leading some into false security believing a lie rather than the truth. In this way, Satan gives men a feeling of security without the need to surrender to the living God. The following is an example of what some of these teachers are teaching:

> "Richard Niebuhr once said that in all these religious theories and expressions, what we are really looking for seems to be 'a God without wrath who took man without sin into a kingdom without righteousness through the ministrations of a Christ without a cross.' A different way to say the same thing is that we have so deified man and dehumanized God that we can scarcely tell the difference."[7]

> Zacharias adds, "It is the new brash, crude, and vulgar way of desensitizing us to the sacred and deforming our mindset, all in the name of God Talk."[8]

> "In Tolle, you have the erosion of the temporal categories; in Walsch, the erosion of essential categories; and in all the writers of the New Spirituality, ultimately the erosion of moral absolutes. This is a deadly word game at work. Morality, time, essence, absolutes – all gone by the wayside in the name of spirituality ... so, refashion Jesus."[9]

> "There is a clear agenda. In their deep prejudice against Christianity, advocates of the New Spirituality malign the Christ of history in order to remake him into an image that is consistent with their ideas."[10]

Interestingly, Satan's first attack on truth was in the Garden. By implying that God had not been truthful, he placed doubt in

Eve's mind. Whose truth was Eve to believe, God's truth or the serpent's story? After all the fruit looked good, it was attractive, it was desirous, and she discovered it tasted good. How could there be any death to this? After all, it was good. What Eve and Adam discovered, after the fact, was they had believed a lie, and what God said was true indeed.

That same lie is being promoted today by many who seem to speak for God, but in reality, they are talking for the serpent. If what is said does not fit with scripture, then it must be taken as untruth. God's Word is the truth. As Paul said, *Let God be true, and every man a liar* (Romans 3:4). It is essential that we know where to find the truth. Jesus told his disciples, *Take heed that no man deceive you. For many shall come in my name, saying, I am Christ; and shall deceive many* (Matthew 24:4-5). Jesus also said, *Behold, he is in the desert; go not forth: behold, he is in the secret chamber: believe it not* (Matthew 24:26). This same scheme is being used today to deceive people into thinking that God, Jesus, or an angel is speaking and giving messages to share with the world. Whether it is someone saying, Jesus is in a certain place or a person claiming to be speaking for Jesus, or God, the message is the same – believe it not.

There are those who say because they have seen a great light, and received a new message from God that they are true. Paul points out that we are not to be deceived by anything that is presented as a new message or revelation. His message to the Corinthians who were struggling with false teachers is relevant for us today.

> *But I fear, lest by any means, as the serpent beguiled Eve through his subtilty, so your minds should be corrupted from the simplicity that is in Christ. ... For such are false apostles, deceitful workers, transforming themselves into the apostles of Christ. And no marvel; for Satan himself is transformed into an angel of light* (2 Corinthians 11:3, 11:13-14).

James Rutz states in his book, *Megashift,* a George Barna survey that shows the vast majority of Christians think all truth is "situational" that there is no such thing as "absolute moral truth."[11]

Donald Walsch's comments on truth in *Conversation with God:*

> "There is no truth except the truth that exists within you; everything else is what someone is telling you. ... Truth is created, not discovered!"[12]

Robert Spencer describes how people develop their own belief of truth in his book, *The Politically Incorrect Guide to Islam:*

> "The idea that believers shape religion is derived, instead, from the fashionable 1960s philosophy of deconstructionism, which teaches that written words have no meaning other than that given to them by the reader. Equally important, it follows that if the reader alone finds meaning, there can be no truth (and certainly no religious truth); one person's meaning is equal to another's. Ultimately, according to deconstructionism, we all create our own set of "truths," none better or worse than the other."[13]

If this is the case, then where do we go to find the truth and is genuine truth a possibility? We, as born again Christians, need to know the source of truth and if our truth is free of error. Are we able to recognize truth without the right foundation to draw on? Jesus said, *I am the way, the truth, and the life* (John 14:6). God is the truth, and God's Word is the truth, any departure from God's Word is an untruth. A half-truth gets so interwoven with a lie that it becomes deadlier by the mix.

The following scripture is what God's Word says about truth:

> *That by two immutable things, in which it was impossible for God to lie* (Hebrews 6:18).

Immutable: God changes not; God cannot lie, absolutely indisputable. God and God's Word are true; it does not change with the times. God's Word does not change just because someone reads into it what they desire it to say.

> *Jesus Christ the same yesterday, and today, and forever.*
> *Be not carried about with divers and strange doctrines*
> (Hebrews 13:8-9).

Just as God's Word does not change, Jesus does not change. What was true yesterday is true today. The scripture says not to be led astray by strange doctrines such as New Age or Eastern religions, or anyone claiming to speak for God.

> *Paul, a servant of God, and an apostle of Jesus*
> *Christ, according to the faith of God's elect, and the*
> *acknowledging of the truth which is after godliness; In*
> *hope of eternal life, which God, that cannot lie, promised*
> *before the world began* (Titus 1:1-2).

> *The coming of the lawless one is by the activity of Satan*
> *with all power and false signs and wonders, and with*
> *all wicked deception for those who are perishing, because*
> *they refused to love the truth and so be saved. Therefore*
> *God sends them a strong delusion, so that they may*
> *believe what is false* (2 Thessalonians 2:9-11 ESV).

The danger of rejecting the truth of God and God's Word is that man will be turned from the truth to believe a lie. A man has the unique ability to rationalize whatever he desires to accept. Man will make his truth to fit his morality regardless of the outcome. God will not change His truth to satisfy the lust of mankind, or to meet social morality. This type of blindness is called "willful blindness" because a man would rather believe a lie than hear the truth. The truth challenges morality and exposes the real intent of the heart.

The apostle Paul gives greater detail of what happens when men choose to reject God, and God's truth, in favor of the god of this world.

> *Professing themselves to be wise, they became fools, and changed the glory of the incorruptible God into an image made like to corruptible man, and to birds, and four footed beasts, and creeping things. Wherefore God also gave them up to uncleanness through the lusts of their own hearts, to dishonor their own bodies between themselves: Who changed the truth of God into a lie, and worshipped and served the creature more than the Creator, who is blessed forever* (Romans 1:22-25).

When men choose to worship and serve the creature, they are choosing an idol to replace the true and living God. Our nation and the world have placed Mother Earth and the environment above God. They have set aside a day to honor Mother Earth, while the teaching of creation has been removed from our schools. The result is nothing more than the humanist religion taking over our schools and teaching their religion as a replacement for Christianity thus setting up a false god and worshiping creation. When men turn away from the truth of God's Word and choose to follow a different path, the enemy of our soul blinds their minds to the truth of God's Word, and they believe a lie.

Several years ago, I was talking with a man about spiritual things. He was explaining to me the value of reincarnation and what a blessing it was to reach Nirvana someday. I responded by telling him what the Bible had to say about the subject, and the need for a new birth to enter heaven.

He said, "Oh, you believe in the Bible."

I said, "Yes."

He then said, "Man wrote that, that is just man's writings."

I asked him, "Who wrote what you believe?"

The man looked startled like that had never entered his mind; however, he insisted that his truth was superior to the Bible.

I believe that the reason men choose to accept the writings of those who say they are speaking for God, and excluding the Bible, is that there is no judgment, and man can write his own ending. Oswald Chambers in his book, *Conformed to His Image*, says, "Nothing is so much resented as the idea that I am not to be my own master. *If anyone desires to come after me, said Jesus, let him deny himself* (Matthew 16:24)."[14]

Walsch and others who claim to be writing, or speaking for God, or giving us messages from God, Jesus, the angels or any other spirit being, are being used by the Devil to lead us into a false religion that undermines the truth of the Bible.

Interestingly, those who speak never mention sin, or judgment, and they teach we can earn salvation by our effort. The lie that deceived Adam and Eve is the same lie used today. Since man is his own god, he is free to write his own rules. He can chart his own course, no need for God or the Bible.

People in the West are flocking to embrace the religion of the East because it offers them the freedom to be a god. By following the teaching passed down by the gurus, a person can reach their full potential. Every discipline is within the power of the individual. "If it is to be, it is up to me." The big "I" is center stage and is self-gratifying, look what I have done.

However, the scripture says, *For by grace are you saved through faith; and that not of yourselves: it is the gift of God: Not of works, lest any man should boast* (Ephesians 2:8-9). It is not by our efforts but by God's grace. Jesus said to Nicodemus, *You must be born again* (John 3:3). Jesus also said, *I am the way, the truth, and the life: no man cometh unto the Father, but by me* (John 14:6). That is the work of the Holy Spirit, not by our efforts.

The truth of God's Word will stand when all other words are proven to be a lie. The scripture says, in speaking of the Devil, *Ye are of your father the devil, and the lusts of your father ye will do. He was a murderer from the beginning, and abode not in the truth, because there is no truth in him. When he speaketh a lie, he speaketh of his own: for he is a liar, and the father of it* (John 8:44).

Erwin Lutzer, in his book, *The Serpent of Paradise,* puts it this way concerning the day in which we are living:

> "He (Satan) will usher in a religion that will counterfeit Christianity at every point. Instead of prayers, there will be mantras; instead of preachers, there will be gurus; in place of prophets, there will be psychics; in the place of the Ten Commandments, there will be new commandments for this new age."[15]

People are searching everywhere for a truth that will satisfy their wants without a commitment to God or God's truth. I like how Major W. Ian Thomas describes the truth in his book, *The Indwelling Life of Christ*:

> "Truth is timeless as God Himself – it never changes. It may be forgotten, neglected, perverted, opposed, rejected, counterfeited, or displaced, but it never changes. Truth is not an emphasis, a concept, a "party line," or merely an option. Truth is imperative. ... Truth does not evolve over the years any more than God evolves, or Christ evolves."[16]

6
Breastplate of Righteousness

. . . having on the breastplate of righteousness . . .

The breastplate is to protect the vital organs. An injury to the vital organs could spell death. It is therefore of utmost importance to protect that part of our spiritual body. Righteousness is knowing what is right and doing it. Righteousness is putting on what God calls righteous, right living, right thinking, right relationships, etc. and making the Bible our guide in all things.

How do we know when we are standing in righteousness? The laws God wrote on tablets of stone are the things God considers sacred, and not to be taken for granted or to be changed to satisfy man's lustful desire. Paul says that Israel rejected God's righteousness and established their own righteousness (Romans 10:3-6). When we reject God's righteousness in favor of our own, we are rejecting God's law and the Word of God as the standard for life. Christ is the fulfillment of the law, in Him, we live; and in Him, we are made righteous.

In reviewing the Ten Commandments, we find that they are just as relevant today as they were the day God gave them to Moses. What God said concerning morality on the mountain, He still says today. His laws are just as holy, and obedience is just as required today as when the law was given. Ravi Zacharias points out that two words "sacred and holy" describe that what God created is sacred, and what God demands is holy. That sums up what righteousness is. What God deems sacred we must treat holy, and that means living a holy life. Hebrews says, *without holiness no man shall see the Lord* (Hebrews 12:14). As for the law, God carved it in stone.

First, God said that there shall be no other gods before Me. He is first, last, and always number one. He is to receive all worship, praise, and glory. God's name should not be taken in vain, that is giving to any other deity or person credit for things that belong to God. Romans chapter one describes what happens when men separate themselves from God and choose to worship the creation rather than the Creator. The message of the New Age movement is "We are god," and since we are god, we can write our own morality. Walsch in speaking for his god says:

> "Most of you, therefore, spend the bulk of your adult life searching for the "right" way to worship, to obey, and to serve God. The irony of all this is that I do not want your worship, I do not need your obedience, and it is not necessary for you to serve Me."[17]

Walsch's god does not want our worship or obedience. That is interesting since I read in Stephen Charnock's book, *The Existence and Attributes of God,* he devoted 70 pages to the subject of worship. I, also read in William Gurnall's book, *The Christian in Complete Armor,* "Nothing hath God kept from his people, saving his crown and glory. That, indeed, he will not give to another (Isaiah 42:8)."[18]

David said, *How good to sing praises to our God! How delightful and how fitting!* (Psalm 147:1 NLT).

God will not take second place to our vocation, recreation, or religion. When anything replaces God in our lives, it becomes an idol to us whether we think it so or not. It may not be an idol of the hand but an idol of the heart, and that is just as damning, separating us from God. Ezekiel tells how the elders of Israel came to the prophet for counsel, and he gives God's response to their idolatry. *Then came certain of the elders of Israel unto me, and sat before me. And the word of the LORD came unto me, saying, Son of man, these men have set up their idols in their heart* (Ezekiel 14:1-3). Just because we don't have a physical image that we sit before and worship, does not mean that we haven't taken into our heart things that replace God.

The Ten Commandments are based on the sacredness of God's creation. God set the boundaries of worship and morality. Morality is what determines right from wrong. Where there is no right or wrong, man has nothing with which to measure his goodness or badness. When we let society set our morality, we have exchanged the morality of God for the morality of man. When we take what God has made sacred or moral, and make it secular, we reject God's righteousness, thus rejecting God, and taking the idols of the world into our hearts. In so doing, we have taken what God has made sacred and made it a sacrilege. God has declared the following as sacred: our nationality, our sexuality, our home, our word, our children, and our worship. When society makes laws based on social pressure and modifies its morality to fit the desire of humanity, God is rejected, and man is exalted. Any rejection of God in favor of the god of this world is idolatry.

By putting on the breastplate of righteousness, we are putting on the Lord Jesus Christ. The more we have of Him, the greater our protection.

7

Shoes of Peace

. . . your feet shod with the preparation of the gospel of peace . . .

Just how important are the shoes? The shoes represent the foundation on which we stand. If our foundation is not secure, there can be no peace. J.I. Packer writes in his book, *Knowing God,* "The peace of God is first and foremost peace with God; it is the state of affairs in which God, instead of being against us, is for us."[19]

I have read different descriptions of soldier's boots, how they help the soldier stand on slippery ground, or how they help him advance. I don't think these descriptions are wrong, but I would like to look at the preparation of peace. If we are to exhibit peace, we must have peace. If we are always in turmoil, we don't have peace.

If we put on peace, like we put on shoes, that will take some thought. There will be some effort involved, that kind of peace doesn't come by itself. We don't just wake up one morning and find that we have peace. We don't prepare for anything without getting involved in the process. In preparing, we grow in knowledge and experience. The more we grow in the knowledge of God and God's Word, the more at peace we become.

Securing peace is a conscious effort; we seek peace on purpose. Peace is learning to rest secure in the midst of a storm. Peace is knowing that no matter how things look at any given moment, God is in control. He will work everything after the counsel of His will (Ephesians 1:11). We have peace even though we don't know all of the facts, or outcome. I believe this kind of peace is developed by going through the storms of life. Each storm is different, and each attack hits us in a different way. As we learn to trust God in each situation, we develop a strength that enables us to trust

God today because we have experienced His deliverance. Each trial helps to build our faith and trust in God.

James gives an example of how we are to respond to trials, *My brethren, count it all joy when ye fall into divers temptations; Knowing this, that the trying of your faith worketh patience. But let patience have her perfect work, that ye may be perfect and entire, wanting nothing* (James 1:2-4). We develop peace by being in the Word and accepting the outcome of each situation as God's best for us. Trusting God for all things that come our way because we know that God knows best and He is on our side no matter how things look. God really has our best interest at heart. Peace grows when we have stood on the scripture and seen God's Word proven to be true.

Many Bible characters come to mind when I think of the victories won by trusting in God: Moses, in delivering Israel out of Egypt. Joshua, in taking Jericho. Gideon, defeating a whole army with three hundred men. David defeated Goliath. Paul and Silas are delivered out of prison. In reading the eleventh chapter of Hebrews, the heroes of faith stand out as examples of God's faithfulness, and the knowledge of God's faithfulness brings peace.

One story I like to reflect on is Queen Esther. It is amazing to watch how God can turn things around when it looks like the die is cast, and there is no way to reverse the situation. Things are not always the way they seem.

Haman, a high ranking official in the king's court, hated one Jewish man, Mordecai. His hatred was so intense that Haman went to the king and secured a decree from the king to kill all of the Jews in the land. Haman so hated Mordecai that a special gallows was built to hang Mordecai. It looked like Haman was on a roll; everything was going his way. But, God had a different plan – Queen Esther. God so reversed the situation that Haman was hung on the same gallows he built for Mordecai. Read the book of Esther and it will bless your heart to see how God works.

With a few examples of God's faithfulness and some personal deliverance, we begin to develop confidence in God that produces peace. Peace grows by immersing ourselves in God's Word and learning to trust God in every situation that comes our way, both the expected and the unexpected. It has been said, when you see a man whose Bible is falling apart – he isn't. Perhaps that says something about his number one priority.

We are in a world filled with chaos, and face difficult problems every day. People are crying for peace, yet there is no peace. Our world is full of people turning to narcotics, alcohol, prescription drugs, Transcendental Meditation, and sex, anything to find peace. "Just make the world go away" is their cry.

Where does the Christian go to find peace? Are Christians turning to the things of the world seeking peace? There is growing evidence that church members are depending on narcotics, prescription drugs, alcohol, and even Hindu practices and New Age religion in the hope of finding peace. They look everywhere but to the God of peace who redeemed them.

The question comes: Why?

What does the scripture have to say about peace?

> *Great peace have they which love thy law: and nothing shall offend them* (Psalm 119:165).

What a powerful verse, having peace, and not being offended by anything. Any time the scripture speaks of the law, it is talking about the scripture, God's Word.

> *For I know the thoughts that I think toward you, saith the* LORD, *thoughts of peace, and not of evil* (Jeremiah 29:11).

There is great comfort in knowing what God thinks of us. Really! God, the Creator of the universe, is thinking of us. I know a lady who was going through a very difficult time. Her world was turned upside down and was falling apart. Every time she spoke, she quoted Jeremiah 29:11. I have had the privilege of seeing how

God has turned a disaster into a blessing. Her life is a glowing example of God's blessing on her and her family.

> *Thou wilt keep him in perfect peace, whose mind is stayed on thee* (Isaiah 26:3).

Nothing takes the place of meditating on the Word of God. On the other hand, Transcendental Meditation is the Eastern religions and New Age method of meditating. Empty the mind and receive from the god of this world, this opens the mind to enemy suggestions that are contrary to the Bible and leads one away from the truth of God's Word.

> *Peace I leave with you, my peace I give unto you* (John 14:27).

Jesus promised us His peace.

Compare the peace of Christ as He faced the cross. He was not free from conflict but was at peace, having full confidence in the outcome. Even when Jesus cried, *My God, My God, why have you forsaken me,* there is no evidence that He questioned why He had to suffer the cross.

> *Be careful for nothing; but in everything by prayer and supplication with thanksgiving let your requests be made known unto God* (Philippians 4:6).

> *And the peace of God, which passeth all understanding, shall keep your hearts and minds through Christ Jesus* (Philippians 4:7).

I like how the New Living Translation reads:

> *Don't worry about anything; instead, pray about everything. Tell God what you need, and thank him for*

all he has done. Then you will experience God's peace, which exceeds anything we can understand. His peace will guard your hearts and minds as you live in Christ Jesus (Philippians 4:6-7 NLT).

Peace comes from a close relationship with God, and an understanding of God's Word. Having on the shoes of peace is not something we can take for granted. That means effort, a plan, and commitment on our part. If we are to put on the shoes of peace, we need to set aside time to put them on. Develop the habit of talking with God daily. One practice that has been helpful to me is meditating on scripture when I wake up at night. I learned that practice from one of my professors at Bible College. That practice usually puts me right back to sleep.

Peace is not the absence of conflict, but it is confidence in God that all is in His hands, and nothing can happen that is outside of His will. Paul said,

All things work together for good to them that love God (Romans 8:28).

Who shall separate us from the love of Christ? Shall tribulation, or distress, or persecution, or famine, or nakedness, or peril, or sword? (Romans 8:35).

For I am persuaded, that neither death, nor life, nor angels, nor principalities, nor powers, nor things present, nor things to come, Nor height, nor depth, nor any other creature, shall be able to separate us from the love of God, which is in Christ Jesus our Lord (Romans 8:38-39).

To have and share the peace, we must take the scripture seriously. Let the Word of God become our beacon. A few of the scriptures that have been a constant in my life are:

Thy word is a lamp unto my feet, and a light unto my path (Psalm 119:105).

Thy word have I hid in mine heart, that I might not sin against thee (Psalm 119:11).

Also, I have found in times of conflict meditating on God's Word is a real source of comfort. The following are a few verses that I have found very helpful over the years: Joshua 1:8; Psalm 1:1-3; Psalm 63:6-7. The more we are in the Word, the more trust we have in God.

So then faith cometh by hearing, and hearing by the word of God (Romans 10:17).

It is by the Word where we gain faith, confidence, trust, security, and peace at all times, and in all situations.

Things that keep a person in bondage to turmoil and unrest are unconfessed sin, an unforgiving heart, and unbelief. Unconfessed sin places a barrier between you and God. As long as that barrier is in place, there will be no peace. Adam and Eve discovered this when they tried to hide from God after sinning.

An unforgiving heart is just as much a barrier, and the tragedy is we become a slave to the one we hold in resentment. Jesus said, *For if ye forgive men their trespasses, your heavenly Father will also forgive you* (Matthew 6:14). Prayer and forgiveness are the keys to peace. No matter the extent of the offense, forgiveness will set you free and bring peace to your soul and your life.

Unbelief will cause a troubled heart. An old saying I heard years ago speaks volumes, "Pray and doubt; you'll do without. Pray and believe; you will receive." If we are in doubt, there is no confidence, no trust, and we fall victim to worry, fear, anxiety, and a troubled heart. Trusting in God and belief in God's Word builds confidence in the believer. With belief and trust in God comes maturity. We mature by growing in the Word, as we apply the Word to our lives.

Make time to pray and spend time with our Lord. Total victory comes when we surrender our will to God – the songwriter said it well.

> You have longed for sweet peace,
> And for faith to increase.
> And have earnestly, fervently prayed;
> But you cannot have rest or be perfectly blest
> Until all the altar is laid.

> Is your all on the altar of sacrifice laid?
> Your heart does the Spirit control?
> You can only be blest
> And have peace and sweet rest
> As you yield Him, your body and soul.

As I think of peace and how we are to share the gospel of peace, I begin to think of a few examples of people who in the middle of suffering found peace. Corrie Ten Boom while in a German concentration camp and Pastor Niemoller while in a German prison for preaching the gospel of Christ are two examples.

Corrie Ten Boom

David Lindstedt in his book, *Faith's Great Heroes*, writes of Corrie Ten Boom and her struggle with betrayal, imprisonment in a concentration camp, her separation from family, and harsh treatment by her captors. Yet, Corrie found in Jesus Christ the strength to forgive and be an encourager to fellow prisoners. Later, she traveled around the world sharing the love of God, and the gospel of peace to a dying world.

Corrie related her struggle when learning the identity of the man who betrayed them to the Nazis. She hated him and then hated herself for hating him. Corrie wondered how she could ever forgive the wretch who caused Papa to die.

"One night she argued about it with her sister Betsie. Betsie had forgiven the traitor, even prayed for him! "Pray for the devil? Never!" said Corrie. ... Corrie forced herself to pray for him too, and for the first time since she learned the man's identity, Corrie slept without bitterness and anger."[20]

Pastor Niemoller

When we are at our lowest, God will send the gospel of peace to comfort us. Erwin Lutzer, in his book, *Hitler's Cross,* describes the story of Pastor Niemoller while in a German prison.

"In 1937, Dr. Niemoller was imprisoned by the Nazis. While in prison awaiting his trial, a green-uniformed official escorted him from his cell to the courtroom. Niemoller described his situation "alone filled with dread and loneliness." Niemoller knew that the outcome was a foregone conclusion. Where were his friends, his family, the members of the Confessing Church?"

"At that moment, he experienced one of the most uplifting experiences of his life as he walked from the cell to the courtroom through an underground passageway. He heard a voice that seemed to be repeating a set of words, but it was so low it was difficult to know where it was coming from because of the echo. Then he realized it was his escort repeating, "The name of the Lord is a strong tower; the righteous run into it and they are safe." Niemoller climbed the steps, his fear was gone, and in its place was the calm brilliance of utter trust in God."[21]

We never know when we will have the opportunity to bring peace to one of God's hurting children. We never know when God will send someone to lift us when we are at the bottom and need to be encouraged. Just because a person is a Christian and has been for a long time doesn't mean that they are always on top of the world. Many times we find ourselves discouraged, lonely, hurting, and we feel that no one cares, and we are sure that God doesn't care either. It is at those times that the gospel of peace speaks volumes to us. Either from an unexpected source or the Word of God; never underestimate the power of the Bible. Erwin Lutzer writes in his book, *The Serpent of Paradise*:

> "There are some battles we cannot fight alone. That is why Paul wrote, *The eye cannot say to the hand, I have no need of you; nor again the head to the feet, I have no need of you* (1 Corinthians 12:21). There are times when the body of Christ must rally behind one of its weakest members."[22]

There are times when as the body of Christ we need to rally around the hurting, lonely, broken, and discouraged members and share the gospel of peace. If we have not put on the shoes of peace, we will not have any peace to share.

8

Shield of Faith

Above all, taking the shield of faith, wherewith ye shall be able to quench all the fiery darts of the wicked.
Ephesians 6:16

"Above all, take the shield of faith" – why above all? Above all means above everything, not a blind faith as some think, but faith based on God's Word that is tried and proven. Everything in our spiritual life depends on faith. If the enemy can cause us to doubt, or question, then he has gained a foothold and will build on it. For an example of the power of doubt, look no further than the Garden of Eden.

The serpent placed doubt in Eve's mind by suggesting that he had a superior truth to what God said. He implied that God was holding something back that would make one wise. By implying that eating the fruit would not cause one to die, but instead, they would become like God. *And the serpent said to the woman, "You surely shall not die! For God knows that in the day you eat from it your eyes will be opened, and you will be like God, knowing good and evil"* (Genesis 3:4-5 NAS). Whenever we doubt the Bible and question, "Is that really what God said?" we are opening the door for Satan to offer his suggestions. Satan's suggestions will always be to satisfy our flesh not the things of God. Questions and doubt usually arise when we desire our will over God's will. In other words, not what God wants, but what I want. This type of questioning is not to be compared with an honest search to find hidden truth in the Word.

The shield of faith is something we build on. The scripture says, we all have a measure of faith. *God hath dealt to every man the measure of faith* (Romans 12:3). If we have a measure, then we must exercise our faith for it to grow. Exercise is pushing against resistance to build our strength. We boast about how we are getting stronger and able to do things we were unable to do before. Yet, we complain when God gives us a trial to help build our faith. David was able to take on Goliath because he had experienced God giving him victory over a bear and a lion. Small victories provide us with confidence as we grow. Then when the big test comes, we can stand strong knowing God will not fail us but will give us victory even when it doesn't seem possible.

Paul admonished Timothy to exercise unto godliness because it was profitable for all things. Exercise unto godliness is exercising our faith.

> *But refuse profane and old wives' fables, and exercise thyself rather unto godliness. For bodily exercise profiteth little: but godliness is profitable unto all things, having a promise of the life that now is, and of that which is to come* (1 Timothy 4:7-8).

As Christians, the enemy wants to divert our focus from Jesus Christ and the Word of God. William Gurnall points out in his book, *The Christian in Complete Armor*:

> "Satan, he will be disputing against this truth and that, to make the Christian, if he can, call them into question, merely because his reason and understanding cannot comprehend them."[23]

We question because we lack understanding or knowledge of the Word. It is of utmost importance that we are in the Word to build our faith. Paul said, *So faith comes from hearing and hearing by the word of God* (Romans 10:17).

Many times when faced with a trial, our natural reaction is to resolve the issue immediately. How often have we found ourselves telling God how to fix the problem, always to our satisfaction, and in the time we desire? God may have a plan that we do not see. Job could not see the reason God allowed Satan to test him. Joseph could not see, at the time, why he was so mistreated. Nevertheless, Job and Joseph never faltered in their faith.

The enemy, if possible, will cause us to take our eyes off God, and doubt His Word. In so doing, we think that we must fix the situation ourselves. The story is told of my father during the Depression in the late 30s. We lived about 20 miles from the town where he worked; he was making about $52.00 a month with six kids in school and two at home. His friends encouraged him to apply for relief, the welfare of the day.

Dad finally decided to sign up and parked the truck, our only means of transportation, in front of the courthouse and was walking up the steps when the scripture came to him. *I have been young, and now I am old; yet have I not seen the righteous forsaken, nor his seed begging bread* (Psalm 37:25). My dad said, "I just turned around and went back to the truck and drove home." In all of the remaining years of the Depression, we never went hungry, without clothing, or a warm place to sleep. God did supply all of our needs, things were tight, but God was faithful to fulfill the needs of His servant.

How does one exercise their faith? Several ways come to mind as I think about this. They are just as difficult to discipline ourselves to do as any discipline is to develop.

A. Being in the Word

One discipline that is hard to develop is to be in the Word of God every day. It is by the Word we are nourished and grow in strength and wisdom. The scripture speaks to all of life and every situation in which we find ourselves. I like what James says concerning trials. Here are three different versions of James 1:2-4 to give a better understanding concerning the different trials and tests that come our way.

King James Version: *My brethren, count it all joy when ye fall into divers temptations; Knowing this, that the* *trying of your faith worketh patience. But let patience have her perfect work, that ye may be perfect and entire, wanting nothing* (James 1:2-4).

English Standard Version: *Count it all joy, my brothers, when you meet trials of various kinds, for you know that the testing of your faith produces steadfastness. And let steadfastness have its full effect, that you may be perfect and complete, lacking in nothing* (James 1:2-4 ESV).

Basic English Version: *Let it be all joy to you, my brothers, when you undergo tests of every sort; Because you have the knowledge that the testing of your faith gives you the power of going on in hope; But let this power have its full effect, so that you may be made complete, needing nothing* (James 1:2-4 BEV).

Other related scriptures are:

All things work together for good to them … who are the called according to his purpose (Romans 8:28).

Greater is He that is in you, than he that is in the world (1 John 4:4).

There hath no temptation taken you but such as is common to man (1 Corinthians 10:13).

Rejoice evermore. Pray without ceasing. In every thing give thanks: for this is the will of God in Christ Jesus concerning you (1 Thessalonians 5:16-18).

But they that wait upon the Lord shall renew their strength; they shall mount up with wings as eagles; they

*shall run, and not be weary; and they shall walk, and
not faint* (Isaiah 40:31).

Being in the Word is more than just having a general knowledge
of the scripture. It is letting the Word feed us our daily bread,
becoming a part of our life. It is where we grow by the Word,
make our decisions based on the Word, develop our morality by
the Word, and the Word secures our foundation. Psalm 119:9-16
gives great instruction on how to grow in the Word.

> *Wherewithal shall a young man cleanse his way? by
> taking heed thereto according to thy word. With my
> whole heart have I sought thee: O let me not wander
> from thy commandments. Thy word have I hid in mine
> heart, that I might not sin against thee. Blessed art thou,
> O Lord: teach me thy statutes. With my lips have I
> declared all the judgments of thy mouth. I have rejoiced
> in the way of thy testimonies, as much as in all riches. I
> will meditate in thy precepts, and have respect unto thy
> ways. I will delight myself in thy statutes: I will not forget
> thy word* (Psalm 119:9-16).

If we were to take these words and apply them to our daily lives,
we would be surprised as to how our faith would grow. Our trust
in God would grow in strength, just like our muscles get stronger
with daily exercise. By disciplining ourselves to meet daily and talk
with our heavenly Father, and letting the Bible become more than
just a book. Taking the Word in as our daily bread will develop
spiritual maturity and a trusting relationship with our heavenly
Father.

B. Prayer

There probably has been more written on the subject of prayer
than any other subject in the Bible. There are books and articles
on intercessory prayer, how to develop a prayer life, great men of

prayer, examples of biblical prayer, why we should pray – the list is endless. The truth is we all know we need to pray, but the discipline is not one we enjoy. It is more difficult than physical exercise, or dieting, and why is that so?

I believe there are a couple of reasons that play into the difficulty of setting aside time to pray.

1. We have an enemy that does not want us to pray because that is the one area where he is defeated. He will throw a dozen situations into our path to hinder us. Some of the things that hinder us are that we are so busy that time gets away from us, and on and on goes the battle.

2. We are not face to face with God; we are in a spiritual relationship. The Spirit is unseen; we want to see to whom we are talking. We enjoy seeing a physical response to our conversation. An immediate answer to our requests is a priority. When we give praise, we want to see the approval of the one receiving it. I believe this is why people turn to symbols, saints, icons, and images because they feel they have a personal audience.

We don't sit down and think about this as being a hindrance to our prayer life, but I believe it does affect us. Jesus said, *That God is a Spirit: and they that worship him must worship him in Spirit and in truth* (John 4:24). As we begin to pray, our inner person reaches out to God, His Spirit connects with our spirit, and we know that we have fellowship with Him. That is where faith comes in; we do not always feel like we have face to face communication with God. Sometimes we feel like we are just talking to the air, there is no feeling, no emotion, seemingly a useless exercise, but it is not.

Oswald Chambers writes in his devotional, *My Utmost for His Highest:*

"At times God will appear like an unkind friend, but
He is not; He will appear like an unnatural father, but
He is not; He will appear like an unjust judge, but
He is not. Keep the thought that the mind of God is
behind all things strong and growing."[24]

God does not give us overcoming life. He gives us life as we overcome. The strain of life is what builds our strength. If there is no strain, there will be no strength.

Faith is a growing process; the more time we spend in prayer, and in the Word, the more our faith grows. We must press in and be diligent in seeking the Lord. It takes discipline to consistently pray. As we do, God becomes more real to us, and we begin to look forward to spending time with Him. I like what Paul said, *Pray without ceasing* (1 Thessalonians 5:17). We can be in a place where we talk with God all day in every situation. These are not long formal prayers, just quick phrases. Whatever comes to mind at the moment, for a situation, a need, praise, or a request. I think of this as having a conversation with God. God is always with us for we are His temple, His Spirit dwells within us (1 Corinthians 3:16). I read this the other day on Facebook; it is worth passing on.

When I am alone, God is my comfort.
When I am nothing, God is my everything.
When I am sad and lonely, God is my song and joy.
When I am weak, God is my strength.

C. Resting in the Word

I believe this is the most difficult of all. Resting is letting go, letting go of our control, letting go of our expectations, surrendering our will to His will. Allowing God to work His plan in our lives to accomplish His good work, that we may be complete, lacking nothing.

Another area of significant hindrance to rest is being still, quietly waiting on the Lord. *Be still and know that I am God* (Psalm 46:10). In our society, being still and listening is not one of our strong suits. We are living in a fast-paced world. Everything is instant. If we have to wait more than a few seconds for the computer to respond, we complain. Microwave ovens cook our meal in minutes or we eat at fast-food restaurants. We are programmed to believe that when we want something we get it with no delay. If our problem is not resolved to our satisfaction, then promptly, we complain and find fault with God.

Not unlike the children of Israel, whose memory of God's deliverance was very short-lived. As long as we are trying to solve our problems, God will not interfere. He will let us struggle and be frustrated. God allowed the children of Israel to have their way but sent leanness into their souls (Psalm 106:15). When we insist on having it our way, we will suffer the consequences or we can surrender our will to God. *We know that all things work together for good to them that love God (Romans 8:28).*

Just reading the Word will not build faith; our faith grows as we internalize the Word. The Word becomes the foundation on which we build our faith. Resting in the Lord is exercising our faith. The scripture supplies us with instruction on resting, standing still, meditating on, and waiting on God, then seeing the salvation of the Lord, God's deliverance. *Be still and know that I am God* (Psalm 46:10). *Thou shall meditate day and night* (Joshua 1:8). *Blessed is the man that heareth me, watching daily at my gates, waiting at the posts of my doors* (Proverbs 8:34). *Take my yoke upon you… For my yoke is easy, and my burden is light* (Matthew 11:29-30). *Having done all to stand. Stand.* (Ephesians 6:13-14). Thus putting on the whole armor of God.

D. Praise and Worship

Praise and worship are not just a Sunday thing that happens in the church. Praise and worship together are an exercise that we may participate in every day, all day. The scripture says to sing unto the Lord, to meditate on the Word while walking and while on your bed. In speaking of the law, it is in the Word where God gives specific instructions.

> *And thou shalt teach them diligently unto thy children, and shalt talk of them when thou sittest in thine house, and when thou walkest by the way, and when thou liest down, and when thou risest up. And thou shalt bind them for a sign upon thine hand, and they shall be as frontlets between thine eyes. And thou shalt write them upon the posts of thy house and on thy gates* (Deuteronomy 6:7-9).

In other words, memorize scripture. Write scripture on 3X5 cards, and carry them with you, read them throughout the day. Post scripture on your bathroom mirror, and other places where you will see them through the day. Worshiping the Lord will build your faith because it strengthens your relationship with Him. The enemy is ever ready to shoot fiery darts at us, and the shield of faith will counter those darts. Some darts we often don't recognize as being from our enemy are:

> 1. Failed expectations. We all have expectations of things we hope will happen or things we desire. The things we plan for, build toward, or train for, we expect what the outcome will be. When things don't turn out the way we had expected, our world falls apart. It is at this time the enemy comes with a truckload of emotions telling us how unfair life is and that we should fight back to achieve the goal we thought we deserved.
> Taking up the shield of faith is surrendering our will to God's will and resting in the fact that God knows best and that His plan will be to our benefit. *And we know that all things work together for good to*

55

them that love God (Romans 8:28). Let faith bring peace during the storm. *Casting all your care upon Him; for He careth for you* (1 Peter 5:7).

2. **Discontentment is a huge factor that hinders our faith.** Hebrews says, *Let your conversation be without covetousness; and be content with such things as ye have: for he hath said, I will never leave thee, nor forsake thee* (Hebrews 13:5). In our world of pressure, we are less content with what we have. We are reaching for more – more money, better homes, newer cars, more toys, the list is endless. When we become content in Christ, we allow Him to fill our life, instead of turning to the world. Jesus said, *But seek ye first the kingdom of God, and his righteousness; and all these things shall be added unto you* (Matthew 6:33).

3. The spirit of bitterness is a deep-seated ill will toward an injustice, or perceived injustice that occurred in our past. The enemy is ever ready to bring up our past and remind us of mistreatment. As long as we hold on to the past, we will be held captive by it. Freedom comes when we forgive the wrongs done to us and accept what Christ has done. When we consider what Christ suffered at the hands of his enemies yet said, "Father, forgive them," can we do any less? Forgive those who have wronged us in the past, whether in person or in the spirit, which will bring us complete victory, and peace of mind. Sometimes it is impossible to go back into our past, but we can forgive in our hearts, and that is just as effective.

4. Unresolved issues can negatively affect relationships. They do not fade away unless you

make an effort to work through them. Whether your unresolved issues originate from disappointments in the past or are in a present relationship, you should not remain enslaved to them. Unresolved issues may be the most difficult to overcome. Over a lifetime, many relationships become stormy, or downright bitter. Getting past the hurts and emotions that are connected to those unresolved issues can be very challenging. That is the time to commit everything to God, casting all of your cares upon Him, then rest in Him.

I heard an illustration given one time on casting all of our cares on Christ that seems fitting here. Get a chair and place it in front of you. Pick up a pillow, hold it in your hand. The chair represents Christ; the pillow represents your cares. Tell God that you are casting your cares upon Him and throw the pillow into the chair. In so doing, you are casting your cares upon Christ. Learn to leave them there and don't take them up again. 1 Peter 5:7 says, *Casting all your care upon him; for he careth for you.*

5. Hidden motives and secret sins play a large part in how we relate to God which affects our relationship, therefore our faith. Sometimes, we get involved in a program that someone has promoted and feel that it is a worthy project. It may be a worthwhile program, but is it God's plan for you? The focus soon turns to "what can I get?" not "what does God want?" Be careful about jumping in until you know the purpose behind the program.

Another area the enemy can trap us is a sin that is not open but private. No matter what it may be, it can render us ineffective for Christ. An example of secret sin is internet porn. This can become so addictive that it will take concentrated prayer and determination to break the addiction. When caught in such a sin, we may need help to break the power of that sin. That is the time to seek help from a pastor, friend, or counselor to gain freedom and victory, defeating the enemy. Also, stand on the scripture, *If we confess our sin, He is faithful and just to forgive us our sins, and to cleanse us from all unrighteousness* (1 John 1:9).

6. Rebellion, the spirit of rebellion, is not a small thing. *For rebellion is as the sin of divination, and presumption is as iniquity and idolatry* (1 Samuel 15:23 ESV). In our society, rebellion is accepted as a normal act. From the revolution of the sixties, our culture is a rebellious one. Rebellion is telling God that we don't need Him; we are going to do it our way. That is the sin that caused Satan to be ejected from heaven (Isaiah 14:12-14).

7. Pride is an inwardly directed emotion that carries two opposing meanings. With a negative connotation, pride refers to a foolishly and irrationally corrupt sense of one's value, status, or accomplishments. With a positive connotation, pride refers to a humble and content sense of attachment toward one's own or another's choices and actions, or toward a whole group of people. It also is a product of praise, independent self-reflection, and a fulfilled feeling of belonging.

8. Tearing others down, gossiping, etc. is a spirit of destruction. A get-even spirit is, "I am going to pay back for wrongs done to me." We demand our rights, and we are not going to rest until we get satisfaction.

Never mind what the scripture says, *Avenge not yourselves … For it is written, Vengeance is mine; I will repay saith the Lord* (Romans 12:19). When we surrender our rights to God and trust Him, He will always properly defend us and bring glory to His name.

These are things that creep into our lives and can have a devastating effect when we realize that our desire to be in the Word has cooled. That is the time to examine ourselves to see what has pushed the love for God and His Word into the background. We need to ask God to forgive us and return to the task of building our faith in God and His Word. In the book of Revelation, John records that the church of Ephesus had lost their first love. They were admonished to repent and return to do the deeds they did at first (Revelation 2:1-5).

Standing on the promises is dead if those promises are severed from Christ. Just reciting the words in scripture are mere words unless they are connected to Christ by faith. *If ye abide in me, and my words abide in you, ye shall ask what ye will, and it shall be done unto you* (John 15:7). The key is abiding. *Take my yoke upon you, and learn of me; for I am meek and lowly in heart: and ye shall find rest unto your souls. For my yoke is easy, and my burden is light* (Matthew 11:29-30). *Be not deceived; God is not mocked: for whatsoever a man soweth, that shall he also reap. For he that soweth to his flesh shall of the flesh reap corruption; but he that soweth to the Spirit shall of the Spirit reap life everlasting.* (Galatians 6:7-8).

Andrew Murray, in his book, *The Believer's Prayer Life,* says that we either live to please our flesh or we live to please God.

> "Scripture teaches us that there are only two conditions possible for the Christian. One is a walk according to the Spirit, the other a walk according to "the flesh." These two powers are in irreconcilable conflict with each other."[25]

59

The obedience of faith is as Paul says, *I live; yet not I, but Christ liveth in me: and the life which I now live in the flesh I live by the faith of the Son of God, who loved me, and gave himself for me* (Galatians 2:20).

While driving through the Rockies as I was touring through Northwestern Montana, I was impressed by the mountains' sheer rock walls that extended upward for thousands of feet. As I thought of this, I began to think that no matter how severe the storms that come against the mountain, or how long the clouds hide it from view, when the storm ceased, and the clouds passed, the mountain remained unmoved.

Jesus told about the wise man who built his house on the rock, the Word of God. Staying anchored to the foundation no matter how severe the storm, no matter how dark the clouds that block our view. When we keep our focus on Jesus Christ and the Word of God, we will not be moved. That is faith in action. That is taking, and using the Shield of Faith.

9

The Helmet of Salvation

. . . And take the helmet of salvation . . .

Why the helmet of salvation? What does salvation have to do with defensive armor? Salvation is the crowning piece of armor, without the helmet the other pieces are ineffective.

By putting on the helmet of salvation, we have surrendered our lives to Christ. We have become a new creation, citizens of heaven; we are no longer a part of this world. We are in the world but not of the world (John 17:11-16). That is what makes our battle with the principalities, powers, and spiritual wickedness more acute because the enemy hates God and anyone or thing that represents God. When we receive Christ, we place Him first in our lives, giving Him the authority to take control, thus setting Him as our head. Putting on the helmet of salvation puts the Holy Spirit, who is our guide, comforter, helper, and teacher, in the control center of our lives.

The helmet protects the head where the control center of the body resides. Man's brain is an amazing part of the body, for that is where the mind is. Man doesn't do anything externally that doesn't pass through the mind first. The mind is also the storage center of every event that we encounter; whether physical, mental or emotional.

Information is first processed by the mind to separate truth from error. Morality is first processed by the mind to determine if it is God's morality or secular morality. No wonder the scripture says stand still before moving ahead or responding to any given situation. The mind is where the battle is won or lost.

With the helmet of salvation, we have the mind of Christ (1 Corinthians 2:16). Billy Graham commenting on the mind of

Christ, said, "Jesus had the most all-encompassing mind this world has ever seen." He goes on to say that "Jesus was so confident in His mind that He could mingle with anyone, or group and not be swayed in His standing with the Father."[26] When Jesus was faced with temptation, He stood on the truth of God's Word. It is paramount that we stay in the Word when faced with any testing. Measure everything with the Word, and the Holy Spirit will give us the wisdom to judge correctly.

If Satan can, he will attack the mind first, causing us to doubt the truth of what God has said. I thought about the serpent and Eve in the garden. I began to picture how Satan works, his tactics haven't changed. I imagine Eve standing in the garden looking at the forbidden tree and thinking about what God had said. As she was standing there, the serpent approached her, saying, "What are you doing?" She responded, "Nothing."

The serpent then began engaging her in conversation about the garden and all of the fruit. She responds, "But not all of the fruit." The discussion continues until Eve says, "We are not to eat or touch the tree in the midst, or we will die." The serpent then encouraged her to look more closely at the tree, "See how pleasant it is." He continued saying, "God knows that the fruit will make you wise, and you will be like God. See how shiny it is, how can anything that desirable be wrong? Touch the leaves see how smooth and soft they are. Feel the fruit, doesn't it feel comforting, take a bite it won't hurt, just a little bite. You really won't die; God didn't mean what He said, that was just a misunderstanding." Eve's mistake was buying into what the serpent said, rather than comparing it to what God said.

When the mind is under attack regarding truth or morality, it will never be a frontal attack. It will always be subtle, little steps, small injections to cause doubt. Things may sound reasonable, but are they based on scripture? All new thought and new interpretation must agree with the Word of God. Are there subtle changes to the Word, has the meaning been altered from the original? Just because something sounds plausible does not make it true.

When faced with a moral issue, Satan always tempts with things that satisfy the flesh, the eye, or pride (1 John 2:16). Things the natural man desires or feels that he needs. There may be some very reasonable needs that the enemy is using to get our eyes away from our objective. A quick fix to the situation, could be a good solution and has worked for others, but is it the plan that God has for us? It's time to stand still and see the salvation of the Lord. In dealing with the flesh, when the eye wanders, our lustful nature is stimulated. The enemy comes alongside and suggests try it; you'll like it, a little won't hurt, you can always stop or change your mind later. How many of us have fallen for such a line?

A personal experience: A few years ago, my wife and I were at a restaurant enjoying an afternoon meal. After lunch before leaving, we stopped at the restrooms. I came out before my wife and was standing by the restrooms waiting for her. While waiting, I was looking out toward the windows when two ladies stepped up between me and the doors leading onto the deck. One lady had on slacks, and the other was wearing a dress. I found myself looking at the lady in the dress to see if I could see through her dress. When it dawned on me what was happening, I said to myself, "What are you doing?" I immediately stopped, turned around and said, "God, forgive me." We must always be on guard to protect our minds, by what we see and hear.

Our mind is a precious part of our body, and we must protect it at all costs. We must fill our minds with the Word of the Lord and meditate on the Word day and night, so the enemy has no place to get a foothold. What we see, we cannot un-see. What we hear, we cannot un-hear. What we read, we cannot un-read. What we put into our mind goes into our heart, thus becoming the desire of our heart.

Watch where you are looking because where you look is where you will end up. Keep your eyes on Jesus, the goal, the prize, heaven, eternity. Remember death is not the end, heaven is real, and eternity is forever.

When I was learning to drive my father said to me, "You keep your eyes on the road because you drive where you are looking." I never forgot that advice and have found it to be good advice in all of life. In protecting the mind, the eyes have a large part to play. The writer of Hebrews says, *Looking unto Jesus, the author, and finisher of our faith* (Hebrews 12:2). The New International Version (NIV) says, *Let us fix our eyes on Jesus, the author and perfecter of our faith* (Hebrews 12:2 NIV). If we keep our eyes on Jesus, there is less chance that the enemy will gain a foothold in our minds.

The scripture tells us what and how to think. There are many passages of scripture that if followed, will help build in us the mind of Christ. Paul says, *To renew our minds* (Romans 12:2). The following is a list of scriptures that can strengthen the helmet of salvation:

Thou wilt keep him in perfect peace, whose mind is stayed on thee: because he trusteth in thee (Isaiah 26:3).

Thou shalt love the Lord thy God with all thy heart, and with all thy soul, and with all thy mind (Matthew 22:37).

For who hath known the mind of the Lord, that he may instruct him? But we have the mind of Christ (1 Corinthians 2:16).

And be not fashioned according to this world: but be ye transformed by the renewing of your mind (Romans 12:2 ASV).

And be renewed in the spirit of your mind; And that ye put on the new man, which after God is created in righteousness and true holiness (Ephesians 4:23-24).

If there be therefore any consolation in Christ, if any comfort of love, if any fellowship of the Spirit, if any bowels and mercies, Fulfill ye my joy, that ye be likeminded, having the same love, being of one accord, of one mind. Let nothing be done through strife or vainglory; but in lowliness of mind let each esteem others better than themselves. Look not every man on his own things, but every man also on the things of others. Let this mind be in you, which was also in Christ Jesus (Philippians 2:1-5).

Finally, brethren, whatsoever things are true, whatsoever things are honest, whatsoever things are just, whatsoever things are pure, whatsoever things are lovely, whatsoever things are of good report; if there be any virtue, and if there be any praise, think on these things (Philippians 4:8).

It is said, that the battle is either won or lost in the mind. The whole world understands the power of the mind, and they seek to regulate its power. Self-help teachers, motivational teachers all teach the importance of mind control. Eastern religions teach control of the mind through Transcendental Meditation. The Law of Attraction teaches whatever you desire – fix your mind on it – and the universe will bring it to you. All self-help books are based on the power of the mind. If it is to be, it is up to me. What the mind can conceive and believe it can achieve. There are hundreds of books describing how to give the mind power, but few follow the teaching of scripture.

What influences our thinking? The books we read and the people we associate with will determine the person we will become. *Be not conformed to this world, but be transformed by the renewing of our mind* (Romans 12:2). When we conform, we are conforming to outside pressure allowing the world to squeeze us into their mold. Being transformed is allowing God to change us from the inside out, by the renewing of our mind. Feed on the living Word of God. Renewing our mind is another word for renovating, completely remodeling the old and making it new. If you let Christ live in your heart, He will do the fighting for you. If Christ is just a resident and you are the one in charge of your own affairs, you will be in a constant state of turmoil. We must die to self as Paul teaches in the book of Romans.

Christ doesn't halfway clean the heart – it is all or nothing. Moses didn't take part of the people out of Egypt – it was all or none. When we surrender our all to Christ putting on the whole armor of God, how we use each piece of armor will develop as we mature. All pieces of the armor must be intact, or there will be a breach giving the enemy an opening.

A breach will cause a weakness in our spiritual life. When love cools, obedience falters. When obedience falters, faith weakens. When faith weakens, hope is weakened. When hope is weakened, we are a sitting duck for the enemy to attack with his various flaming arrows. It is, therefore, imperative that we stay in a close relationship with our heavenly Father. We must know His Word, and live by His Word, no matter the situation. Our battle is an eternal battle, a battle with the arch-enemy of our souls.

10

Sword of The Spirit

. . . and the sword of the Spirit, which is the word of God . . .

Of all of the armor, the sword is the only piece that we are to use against the enemy. When Jesus was tempted by the Devil in the wilderness, his only weapon was the Word of God. He said, "It is written." He never changed His response. Jesus never discussed the situation or explained His reason. Jesus just said, "It is written."

The Bible says, the Word of God is quick and powerful, and sharper than any two-edged sword. Therefore, the enemy will go to any length to minimize its effect. People don't want to hear what the Bible has to say about morality or submission to God. The Bible has been repeatedly attacked throughout history. Since the 1960s in America, we have seen an increase in attacks on the Bible and Christian values. First, the Bible was removed from the schools, then the Ten Commandments removed from public locations. Then society deemed their morality superior to that of the Bible. When psychology replaced the word "sin" with the words, "sickness" and "disease" mankind no longer accepted responsibility for their actions, and they became victims. It is always someone else's fault. With the Bible pushed into the closet, we have watched our nation plunge deeper and deeper into a moral freefall.

With the Word put comfortably out of sight, because it may offend someone, or make them feel bad, the enemy has gained a foothold in diminishing the strength of the Word, thus making it easier for the enemy to inject his deceptions. Some tricks of the enemy are very subtle, while others are direct. The subtlety of Marcus Borg, Professor of Religion at Oregon State, in his book, *Reading The Bible Again for the First Time*, as he explains that the

Bible is not to be taken literally, but seriously. He presents the Bible as a book of allegory. Meaning the writers used a device or character that is symbolic, rather than literal. His thesis of taking the Bible seriously, but not literally, undermines the truth of scripture. The concept is if it doesn't fit with science and logic, then science and logic must be the final authority.

Modern theologians love to manipulate people by redefining words and giving them a meaning directly opposite of what the words historically denoted. Thomas C. Oden, a theological professor, writes, "In my seminary teaching I appeared to be relatively orthodox ... the trick was to learn to sound Christian while undermining traditional Christianity."[27] And he adds, the theologian's task was to deconstruct old religions to create a new religion. The Bible says, *The time will come when they will not endure sound doctrine; but after their own lust shall they heap to themselves teachers, having itching ears* (2 Timothy 4:3).

The Bible has been under attack from educational, political, and social realms to destroy the cutting edge of the sword because *the Word of God is quick, and powerful, and sharper than any two-edged sword, piercing even to the dividing asunder of soul and spirit, and of the joints and marrow, and is a discerner of the thoughts and intents of the heart* (Hebrews 4:12).

The Word of God can cut to the heart of the matter in just a few words. I remember reading a book by D.L. Moody years ago. I don't remember the name of the book, but one thing I do remember is what he said about how he used scripture. Moody said, "When I meet a man who does not believe the Bible, I just quote the scripture." I took that statement to heart and have lived by it. I do not have to defend the Bible; all I have to do is quote it.

How should we care for our sword? Can you conceive of anyone who has a sword to protect themselves from an enemy taking it casually? They would guard it, polish it, sharpen it, and learn how to use it. Is the sword of the Spirit any different? Should we not spend time learning what the Word says, and how to apply it to any given situation? The Bible is a literal book, the events of the

Bible are real, the message of the Bible is eternal, and any attempt to make it less is of the Devil, our enemy.

The gospel of John opens with, *In the beginning was the Word, and the Word was with God, and the Word was God. The same was in the beginning with God. All things were made by him; and without him was not anything made that was made* (John 1:1-3). Jesus was at the beginning with God, Jesus was instrumental in creation, Jesus is eternal, and He is the Word of God. When we take the sword of the Spirit, we are taking Jesus as our defender, and He will never fail us. Jesus said, *Heaven and earth shall pass away, but my word shall not pass away* (Matthew 24:35). Isaiah says, *The grass withereth, the flower fadeth: but the word of our God shall stand forever* (Isaiah 40:8). Peter adds, *But the word of the Lord endures forever* (1 Peter 1:25).

The events that the Bible describes are literal events. God literally created the world and everything in it. God literally delivered Israel out of Egypt. God literally opened up the Red Sea for Israel to cross over on dry ground. God literally delivered Jonah out of the belly of a great fish. God literally delivered Daniel from the lions and his three friends out of the fiery furnace. Jesus literally came to earth, was crucified, was buried, and rose from the grave on the third day. He ascended into heaven. And He is literally coming back again.

God's Word will stand forever; it is our rock, our solid foundation, and they who build on it will not be shaken. Within the law of God, there are boundaries, parameters, guidelines, restrictions, and instruction; you want to enjoy life, honor God's Word and His commandments, do it His way. The enemy says to do away with boundaries, parameters, and guidelines; do your own thing. Any departure from the Bible is a departure from truth. Never try to defend the Word, let the Word speak for itself, and it will cut to the heart of any situation. If a person is determined to be an unbeliever, nothing you can add will change their mind, and it will only cause them to cling more tightly to their unbelief. Stand on the Word, live by the Word, and whenever the enemy attacks, we will not be shaken, we will stand secure.

11

Praying Always

Praying always with all prayer and supplication in the
Spirit, and watching thereunto with all perseverance and
supplication for all saints.
Ephesians 6:18

Paul concludes this section on the armor of God with instructions to pray. In praying always, there is no set time to pray, always be in tune with God. Whenever the need arises, pray. I have found that when people ask me to pray for them or a particular situation, I stop at that moment and pray. I don't do my devotions, I pray for the need. Too often the response is I will pray about it, only to forget at a later time. Paul also said, *Pray without ceasing* (1 Thessalonians 5:17). We are to be in constant connection with our heavenly Father. I like what our pastor said about prayer. He said prayer is like texting. We send quick short messages all the time. We need that kind of relationship with God, always speaking our needs, praises, and thankfulness in quick short prayers to our heavenly Father. That does not take away from the need to have a set time of prayer and devotion.

Supplication

There are several adjectives that help us to understand what Paul is saying. They are:

1. Sincere, not half-heartedly, but understanding the seriousness of the need.

2. Honest, being honest with ourselves, not trying to sugarcoat the situation. God knows the truth, and we

need to accept the truth regardless of the pain, the embarrassment, or the shame we feel.

3. Straight forward, no beating around the bush. Get to the point, Jesus encouraged us to pray a specific type of prayer when He gave the Lord's Prayer as an example (Matthew 6:9-13).

Watching

Be alert, pay attention; don't get taken by surprise. We are in a war with the enemy of our soul and should never be caught off guard. I don't mean to say that we should be looking for the enemy under every bush, but we should always be alert. Be alert to the need of our fellow Christians when they are going through a tough time.

The code of the military is, no person will be left behind, which should be our code, as Christians. We must pray for each other and be an encourager to one another. All of us face battles and we need help. Knowing that someone is in our corner is a great help and comfort during these times.

With Perseverance

With perseverance means with urgency, resolve, determination. We are not in a short war; we are in an eternal battle. It is therefore of utmost importance that we don't lose heart and give up. Paul admonishes us, *be not weary in well doing: but in due season we shall reap, if we faint not* (Galatians 6:9). We are to be overcomers, as we strive for the crown of life. We have heaven to gain and hell to avoid. We are anchored to the rock that cannot be moved; our anchor holds no matter the storm or trial.

Considering that Paul's instruction is to put on the whole armor of God, and concludes with prayer is significant. In every war, there is a chain of command. There is always someone at the top who knows what is going on and given the authority to direct the soldier on the front line. When we pray, we accept the authority of God. We don't question His word, we submit to it; prayer is the first step of surrender.

When I joined the military, in one of the first classes, we received General Orders. These orders were given to every recruit and were expected to be followed precisely as presented, not to follow them brought severe consequence. These orders were to teach us how to respond if taken by an enemy, how to conduct ourselves while on duty, and how to interact with our superiors.

Paul has given us a list of general orders to help us in our war with the enemy of our soul. We may skip over them taking the ones we like and leaving the rest. We may take them for granted or take them seriously. Paul spells out that we are in a cosmic war with the god of this world. He instructs us to put on the whole armor of God to be equipped to withstand his attacks. We are instructed to take the girdle of truth and put on the breastplate of righteousness. We are to put on the shoes of the gospel of peace and to take the shield of faith with the helmet of salvation. He then adds, take the sword of the spirit which is the Word of God, and ends with the command to pray always.

These are not just suggestions to use if the mood hits us or to fall back on when things get too tough for us to handle, this is vital for our survival. Too often we think that we can handle the situation ourselves, when the truth is we need the help of the Holy Spirit at all times.

Speak the Word in prayer to defeat the enemy. The Word of God is a living book. Use it in prayer, and it will cut to the heart, raising a standard against the enemy.

Remember, when Jesus was being tempted, He spoke the Word. We are to use the Word, and speak the Word, stand on the Word, live by the Word. We are to rely on the Word for it is a living book that has stood for all time and it will stand until Jesus comes.

If we expect to hear from God, we best get in the habit of standing on His Word and following His instruction. When we stand on His Word rather than trusting our own understanding, we can pray with confidence. The writer of Proverbs says, *Trust in the LORD with all thine heart; and lean not unto thine own understanding. In all thy ways acknowledge him, and he shall direct thy paths* (Proverbs 3:5-6). When we trust our understanding, we pray with a closed mind. What we are saying is, "God, this is my plan, and I want you to bless it."

We will never go wrong when we choose to stand on the Word of God no matter the situation. God will honor His Word and supply all of our needs. Jesus said, *But seek ye first the kingdom of God … and all these things shall be added unto you* (Matthew 6:33). He never said all of your wants, but all of your needs. *Behold the fowls of the air: for they sow not, neither do they reap, nor gather into barns; yet your heavenly Father feedeth them. Are ye not much better than they?* (Matthew 6:26). The truth of God's Word will stand when all the wisdom of this world passes away.

12

The Battle Continues

Having received instruction on how and why to put on the whole armor of God, we are now instructed to engage in the battle with the spiritual rulers of this world, specifically the principalities, powers, rulers of darkness, and spiritual wickedness. As we look at the signs around us and compare them with what the Bible says concerning the end times, we must more and more be on the alert to the enemy's attacks. Satan has an invading army taking over our culture by lies, deceit, deception, and intimidation, to cause us to capitulate rather than stand firm.

In this world of uncertainty, there are some things that you can count on. In our world of "political correctness", we hesitate to speak for fear of offending someone or making them feel uncomfortable. I am compelled to speak because of the importance of the outcome. There are at least two certain events that each person will face regardless of their belief or political persuasion. The two events that each person will face, prepared for or not, are death and eternity. ***It is appointed unto men once to die, but after this the judgment*** (Hebrews 9:27).

We hesitate to speak of the future because we are so taken up with the present. Death is inevitable, and eternity is certain whether we believe it or not. The Bible says there are two places prepared for man after death. The average person doesn't like to think of this because it may be uncomfortable. By not thinking about the future, we chose to believe "out of sight, out of mind." We are so taken up with the now that we push the inevitable out of our minds hoping that will make it go away, or at least to a more convenient day.

I have watched our country slip more and more into a godless society. We have come from a nation that declared itself a Christian nation to a government that openly declares itself anti-Christian. From the end of World War II, we, as a nation, have systematically pushed God and anything that speaks of God, and Christianity out. And in its place have embraced the humanistic doctrine, specifically the love of self, money, materialism, and hedonism. As a result, we have produced a nation of self-centered, narcissistic people. They are either entitled or victims; in either case, they are not responsible for their actions. We are living in what the Bible calls the end times. There are more signs today than at any time in the history of mankind. We are running headlong into eternity without giving any thought as to where we will end up. This is the battle we are engaged in as Christians.

With a nation that is hell-bent on removing anything that speaks of God and the Bible from society, what are we to do? There has been a concentrated effort to remove the Ten Commandments from every public place, including our schools.

As I reflected on the situation we are facing, I asked myself, how do the Ten Commandments fit into our world today? To my surprise, I found that they are very relevant. The first four commandments deal with man's relationship with God. The last six, deal with man's relationship with men and the community where we live. If our enemy can diminish our relationship with God, he can destroy our relationship with our fellow man. God has not changed His mind or His original laws. As we look at the commandments, it is not hard to see that they are under attack from every direction. The goal is to remove them and God from our society and replace them with the gods of this world.

With that thought in mind, let's take a new look at the Ten Commandments.

13

What God?

Thou shalt have no other gods before me.
Exodus 20:3

Our enemy is actively presenting us with multiple gods to replace the living God of the Bible. I want to point out some of the replacement gods we are embracing. These substitute gods are presented with such subtlety that we don't recognize them as replacing God. One of the most diabolical replacements is our government in the form of socialism. Socialism is the idea that we all accept what society deems correct. Never mind that socialism rejects anything that has to do with biblical values. The government becomes God presenting their world view, and all other views must be suppressed and rejected. In Dietrich Bonhoeffer's book, *The Cost of Discipleship*, he describes socialism as a devilish power designed to overthrow a government.

> "The fanatical devilish forces within National Socialism left no alternative. They were aiming at the destruction of Germany as a European and Christian country."[28]

> "Both modern liberal theology and secular totalitarianism hold pretty much in common that the message of the Bible has to be adapted, more or less, to the requirements of a secular world. No wonder, therefore, that the process of debasing Christianity as inaugurated by liberal theology led, in the long run, to a complete perversion and falsification of the essence of Christian teaching by National Socialism."[29]

Dietrich points out that National Socialism and liberal theology led to the destruction of Christianity in Germany. Looking at what the enemy has accomplished in Europe, it is not too much of a stretch to see that same pattern being repeated in America. The question is, is the church falling for the same destructive ideas and practices?

Entertainment, sports, pleasure, money, and power, all find their way into the heart of Americans to take God's place. If you couple that with the church retreating from preaching holiness, the cross, and a coming judgment, people are left with a feel-good religion, but no power to transform lives. In Paul's letter to Timothy, he describes what the last days will look like.

> *This know also, that in the last days perilous times shall come. For men shall be lovers of their own selves, covetous, boasters, proud, blasphemers, disobedient to parents, unthankful, unholy, Without natural affection, trucebreakers, false accusers, incontinent, fierce, despisers of those that are good, Traitors, heady, high minded, lovers of pleasures more than lovers of God; Having a form of godliness, but denying the power thereof* (2 Timothy 3:1-5).

And again Paul says,

> *Now the Spirit speaketh expressly, that in the latter times some shall depart from the faith, giving heed to seducing spirits, and doctrines of devils* (1 Timothy 4:1).

According to Dave Reagan of *Lamb & Lion Ministries*, humanism is the religion of Satan teaching that man is capable of fixing all of his problems by himself.

In 1933, thirty-four humanists gathered together to write the radical Humanist Manifesto I. They were professors of Church History and Theology, Harvard University and Tufts College. I was shocked to learn that many Unitarian ministers were among the delegates. They put together 15 statements designed to undermine Christianity and remove God entirely from society. The Manifesto declared itself to be the new religion replacing the old religions of the world.

> "Number Thirteen of the 1933 Manifesto states: Religious humanism maintains that all associations and institutions exist for the fulfillment of human life. The intelligent evaluation, transformation, control, and direction of such associations and institutions with a view to the enhancement of human life is the purpose and program of humanism. Certainly religious institutions, their ritualistic forms, ecclesiastical methods, and communal activities must be reconstituted as rapidly as experience allows, in order to function effectively in the modern world."

The Manifesto came at a time when eugenics philosophy was dominating culture. It rode in on the heels of Hitler's reign of terror in Nazi Germany. What is the eugenic philosophy? Eugenics is the science of improving a human population by controlled breeding to increase the occurrence of desirable heritable characteristics. Developed largely by Francis Galton as a method of improving the human race, it fell into disfavor only after the perversion of its doctrines by the Nazis.

In 1973, 40 years after the first Manifesto was penned, Humanist Manifesto II was drafted. The humanists, eugenicists, and abortion advocates joined forces to write the Humanist Manifesto II. The Humanist Manifesto II was a document written in rejection of orthodox teaching on religion, and the existence of God, and it was signed by several prominent leaders in the abortion movement. They wrote the following:

> "We reject all religious, ideological, or moral codes that denigrate the individual, suppress freedom, dull

intellect, and dehumanize personality. We believe in
maximum individual autonomy . . . the possibilities
of personal *freedom of choice* exist in human life and
should be increased."

"The right to birth control, abortion, and divorce
should be recognized. A civilized society should be a
tolerant one."

In other words, there can be no personal freedom as long as the
concept of God exists, someone that we must answer to now and
in the future (Hebrews 9:27). Man must be free to be whatever he
desires, and there is no right or wrong. It is just what one sees as
right or wrong; everyone dances to their own DNA.

As a civilized society, we should embrace whatever society
decides is right. If you don't agree then you are in the words of
modern society, a hater, homophobe, racist, bigot, and any other
name they can throw at you to make you crawl back into your hole
and speak no more.

The Bible describes the action of our enemy perfectly. *Be sober,
be vigilant; because your adversary the devil, as a roaring lion, walketh
about, seeking whom he may devour* (1 Peter 5:8). Intimidation is
what we are witnessing in our streets, cities, and colleges by those
who hate God, what He stands for, and they hate our nation. I
might add, with the willing help of the media. Thus, they win by
intimidation.

Paul Kurtz, who published Manifesto II in 1973, wrote this in
his preface:

"As in 1933, humanists still believe that traditional
theism, especially faith in the prayer-hearing God,
assumed to love and care for persons…is an unproved
and outmoded faith. Reasonable minds look to other
means for survival."

Manifesto II reinforced the belief that God and religion were to be ignored while human reasoning was to be exalted. It is the lie that the serpent told Eve. You will become like God. The Manifesto goes on to say …

> "We believe… that traditional dogmatic or authoritative religions that place revelation, God, ritual, or creed above human needs and experience do a disservice to the human species … As non-theists, we begin with humans, not God … *Manifesto II* goes on to state that excessive population growth must be checked."

There has been a concentrated effort by the Devil's religion (humanism) to systematically undermine the Christian faith and biblical influence in our society starting with removing the Bible and prayer from our schools and public institutions. According to their manifesto, it says, "We reject all religious, ideological, or moral codes that denigrate the individual, suppress freedom, dull intellect, and dehumanize personality."

The Devil's religion was already heavily involved in attacking the church by questioning biblical morality, the inerrancy of the Bible, and a Holy God that required a holy people was accomplished when the church bought into liberalism. Liberal professors in the universities and preachers began to preach a social gospel, a gospel that did not change lives but gave a good feeling (2 Timothy 4:3). There was no transformation. There was no need to be concerned about serving another god because that new god allowed one to be free to serve themselves, and serve themselves, they did.

The liberal teaching indicates that all content about God, and especially a personal God, is dead. If there is a God, He is removed from mankind and the universe. Not that God was ever alive in their thinking. So every thought about God must be removed for society to function without restraint. The one religion that we have bought into without thinking it was a religion is humanism, the god of the state.

The sexual revelation of the 60s and the hippy movement brought in the advent of free love, drugs, and rebellion – a rejection of all the old established rules and thinking of the previous generations. And on our college campuses, there were riots, the beginning of the great divide in our nation.

As the humanists began to undermine the foundation of America, the Supreme Court began to side with them. Soon after the rebellion of the 60s, the Supreme Court declared that prayer and Bible reading in the public schools were against the Constitution as they saw it. Madalyn Murray O'Hair's challenge drove this decision.

O'Hair is best known for the Murray v. Curlett lawsuit, which led to a landmark 1963 Supreme Court ruling ending official Bible-reading in American public schools. That case came just one year after the Supreme Court prohibited officially sponsored prayer in schools in Engel v. Vitale. The U.S. Supreme Court ruled on June 25, 1962, that voluntary prayer in public schools violated the U.S. Constitution's First Amendment prohibition of a state establishment of religion. It was another step in pushing God out and replacing Him with another god.

This is what the Supreme Court wrote concerning what effect the Ten Commandments might have on the students if they were posted in the schools.

> "Posting of religious texts on the wall serves no such educational function. If the posted copies of the Ten Commandments are to have any effect at all, it will be to induce the schoolchildren to read, meditate upon, perhaps to venerate and obey, the Commandments. However desirable, this might be as a matter of private devotion; it is not a permissible state objective under the Establishment Clause."

It is interesting that the Supreme Court restricted prayer and the Ten Commandants from public schools, yet embrace the Hindu practices of yoga meditation, and allowed Islam to be taught.

Islam is being Taught & Practiced in Public Schools of America!

Brave New Schools: "Five pillars of Islam" taught in public school.

David Fiorazo: Teaches extensively on the rejection of Christianity and the introduction of other religions in the public schools. Check out his website for detailed information: https://www.freedomproject.com/ christ-culture/657-islam-promoted-in-public-schools-christianity-banned

As humanism made more significant inroads into our society, the next milestone was abortion rights. In another landmark decision by the U.S. Supreme Court, Roe v. Wade, the abortion decision in 1973, abortion was legalized. It is also interesting to note that *Manifesto ll* stated that "excessive population growth must be checked." Could this be one of the driving forces behind the abortion movement and the support of Planned Parenthood?

By pushing God out and bringing in other religions, idolatry is introduced into society without looking like idolatry. It sounds so reasonable, just like the serpent in the garden said, "You will not die, you will be like God." The underlying creed of the Manifestos is to reject anything about a Holy God and introduce man as the power to control his destiny. The apostle Paul wrote in the opening chapter of the book of Romans concerning the very times we are living.

Because that which may be known of God is manifest in them; for God hath shewed it unto them. For the invisible things of him from the creation of the world

*are clearly seen, being understood by the things that are
made, even his eternal power and Godhead; so that they
are without excuse: Because that, when they knew God,
they glorified him not as God, neither were thankful;
but became vain in their imaginations, and their foolish
heart was darkened. Professing themselves to be wise, they
became fools, And changed the glory of the incorruptible
God into an image made like to corruptible man, and
to birds, and fourfooted beasts, and creeping things*
(Romans 1:19-23).

When science declares, they know more than their Creator.
When men are capable of fixing their moral differences, and
thinking that all men will agree, as to what is moral without a
change of heart, we have bowed down to a false god.

14
Graven Images

Thou shalt not make unto thee any graven image.
Exodus 20:4

Growing up in America, I never thought that we, as a nation, would ever erect images to idols. However, in just the past few years, we have seen that very thing happen. We have seen the images of false gods displayed and banners hung to honor pagan gods. Plus we have taken the gods of this world into our hearts. In America, a few years ago, we could not have conceived of erecting stone gods to worship. However, on August the 9th, 2015, the Goddess Kali was projected onto the Empire State Building in New York City.

Who is the goddess Kali?
"Kali is the Hindu goddess (or Devi) of death, time, and doomsday and is often associated with sexuality and violence but is also considered a strong mother-figure and symbolic of motherly-love. Kali also embodies shakti – feminine energy, creativity, and fertility – and is an incarnation of Parvati, wife of the great Hindu god Shiva. She is most often represented in art as a fearful fighting figure with a necklace of heads, a skirt of arms, a lolling tongue, and brandishing a knife dripping with blood." For more information see: *Ancient History Encyclopedia*, https://www.ancient.eu/Kali/

The promoter, Android Jones, used the image of Kali because he wanted to provide an incarnation of the Hindu deity in the fight against the harm Earth is enduring by humans today. The image is used in promoting the "Save the Earth" movement – the worship of Mother Earth. It is also interesting that the globalist movement is using the environment as a tool to usher in the one-world government. This religion has spread around the world with global thought given to saving the environment because climate change caused by humans and industry is destroying the world. Men should be respectful of God's creation, but man will not destroy or control nature. The scripture says,

> Lift up your eyes to the heavens, and look upon the earth beneath: for the heavens shall vanish away like smoke, and the earth shall wax old like a garment, and they that dwell therein shall die in like manner: but my salvation shall be for ever, and my righteousness shall not be abolished (Isaiah 51:6).

Are there any temples or worship centers to the goddess Kali in the United States? To my surprise, there is one in Laguna Beach, California.

> Kali temple, Kali Mandir, was formally registered as a California non-profit, tax-exempt religious organization in 1995. Kali Mandir is closely associated with the Dakshineswar Kali Temple, located in Kolkata, India.

Another god was honored in New York City. In September 2016, the gateway to the temple of Baal was unveiled. These images, along with the rainbow flashed on the White House are a flagrant affront to the Christian faith. There is a lot of talk about removing all of the religions of the world, and replacing them with the god of humanism, but what they want is to remove the Christian faith in a living God – thus removing anything that resembles Christ and the Bible.

15

Vain Conversation

Thou shalt not take the name of the Lord thy God in vain.
Exodus 20:7

The concept of taking the Lord's name in vain has traditionally meant using God's name in swearing. I don't think that concept is wrong, but there is more to the commandment than just swearing. Jesus referred to the name of God and the things that belong to God in His sermon on the mountain. He said for man, not to swear or to make an oath by using a name that is holy but to be honest in your conversation.

> *Again, ye have heard that it hath been said by them of old time, Thou shalt not forswear thyself, but shalt perform unto the Lord thine oaths: But I say unto you, Swear not at all; neither by heaven; for it is God's throne: Nor by the earth; for it is his footstool: neither by Jerusalem; for it is the city of the great King. Neither shalt thou swear by thy head, because thou canst not make one hair white or black. But let your communication be, Yea, yea; Nay, nay: for whatsoever is more than these cometh of evil* (Matthew 5:33-37).

I believe Paul gives a perfect example of taking the Lord's name in vain. In Romans, the first chapter, Paul elaborates on the depravity of man, when man rejects the things God created and exalted the creation. He then shows the depth that evil man sinks to when God is rejected (Romans 1:18-32). The Humanist Manifesto is taking everything that God created and declared it to be self-existing, consequently, not giving God credit or honor for His creation. It is obvious that our society doesn't give much thought to taking the Lord's name in vain. To follow the letter of the commandment, one should give more thought as to how we speak and to whom we give praise.

16

A Holy Day

Remember the Sabbath day to keep it holy.
Exodus 20:8

We have taken the Sabbath day and made it a day of commerce. We no longer respect a day as unto the Lord, a day of rest. Sabbath, it's just another day in our life for our pleasure. What the commandment is saying is that we are to set aside one day a week to stop from all labor, and rest our bodies, our minds, and to make it a day to recharge – a day to honor God, to reflect on the blessings of God, and to worship Him. It is to be a time for instruction, to teach our children to respect God and God's laws.

As a child growing up during World War II, life was as different as night and day from today. Sunday was set apart from the other six days of the week. All of the stores in town were closed except for a drug store to meet emergency needs. Sunday was a time for family and friends to get together for lunch after church and an afternoon of relaxing. The day then concluded with a youth meeting and evening service. Not everyone in the community went to church, but most observed the day as a day of rest.

Looking at how we treat the commandments that relate to God speaks volumes as to how we respond to God. Is He first in our lives, or have we replaced Him with the god of humanism? When we successfully replace God with other gods, we take the commandments dealing with our fellow man and rewrite them to suit ourselves. There is no concern given to a judgment day or a time of accountability. Everyone can develop their truth and morals to please themselves, since the God of the Bible is not relevant.

The apostle Paul describes the results of what life is like when God is not recognized in society. When God is replaced with man's reasoning, there are no guidelines where we can point for moral answers. In Romans and Galatians, Paul points out the depravity of mankind when God is rejected. And we wonder where we went wrong.

Because that, when they knew God, they glorified him not as God, neither were thankful; but became vain in their imaginations, and their foolish heart was darkened. Professing themselves to be wise, they became fools, And changed the glory of the incorruptible God into an image made like to corruptible man, and to birds, and four-footed beasts, and creeping things. Wherefore God also gave them up to uncleanness through the lusts of their own hearts, to dishonor their own bodies between themselves: Who changed the truth of God into a lie, and worshipped and served the creature more than the Creator, who is blessed forever. Amen. For this cause God gave them up unto vile affections: for even their women did change the natural use into that which is against nature: And likewise also the men, leaving the natural use of the woman, burned in their lust one toward another; men with men working that which is unseemly, and receiving in themselves that recompense of their error which was meet. And even as they did not like to retain God in their knowledge, God gave them over to a reprobate mind, to do those things which are not convenient; Being filled with all unrighteousness, fornication, wickedness, covetousness, maliciousness; full of envy, murder, debate, deceit, malignity; whisperers, Backbiters, haters of God, despiteful, proud, boasters, inventors of evil things, disobedient to parents, Without understanding, covenant breakers, without natural affection, implacable, unmerciful (Romans 1:21-31).

According to the scripture, it is apparent that we have rejected God. We have become a nation of self-centered people thinking only of what satisfies at the moment. In effect, we have pushed God out of our thinking and replaced Him with the god of humanism. The result: a nation totally in chaos, conflict, and despair.

17

Where Are We on God's Clock?

Looking at all of the divergences that are in the world, it is obvious that Satan has made huge inroads into our country and culture. The question comes, is there any hope for the future, or the Christian? My answer is a resounding "Yes" – provided we keep our eyes on Jesus and stay connected to the Word of God. If we stand firm on the Word and do not compromise our faith, it will not matter what the world does, for our hope is in Christ, not the government. The Bible says, *Be not afraid nor dismayed by reason of this great multitude; for the battle is not yours, but God's* (2 Chronicles 20:15).

God has always stood with those who stood with Him. It does not matter the size of the enemy or how well they are entrenched, God will be the victor. Billy Graham was once asked if he was an optimist or a pessimist. He responded that he was an optimist. When asked why, Billy Graham said, "I have read the end of the book." God will have the last say in world events, and the enemy of our souls will be defeated and thrown into the lake of fire (Revelation 20:10). Until then, we are to keep trusting God and standing on the Word of God.

What does the Bible say the last days will look like? When Jesus was asked what the last days would be like, and what signs would indicate the end, He responded with this discourse in Matthew 24, Mark 13, and Luke 21. His first response was, *Take heed that no man deceive you. For many shall come in my name, saying, I am Christ; and shall deceive many* (Matthew 24:4-5). There have been some who claim to be Jesus, and most Christians recognize them for the deceivers they are. What tricks some Christians is when a person says they are speaking for Jesus, or an angel, saying I have a special message from God. They sound so convincing until you compare what they are saying with the Bible and discover the two don't agree.

Dave Reagan, of *Lamb and Lion Ministries*, highlights six out of fifty end-time signs. The convergence of end-time signs is notable. There has never been a time when all of the signs have come together until now. The six signs are in nature, society, spiritual nature, world politics, technology, and the return of Israel to their homeland. Let's look at each one and see if they speak to us.

Nature

Jesus said, *For nation will rise against nation, and kingdom against kingdom, and there will be famines and earthquakes in various places. All these are but the beginning of the birth pain*s (Matthew 24:7-8 ESV). Nature has been displaying accelerated disasters for the past 20+ years. Fires, earthquakes, hurricanes, and volcanoes all are increasing in frequency and intensity in the last few years. Fire and landslides have destroyed whole communities. Hurricanes and tornados have devastated many communities. Jesus went on to say, the closer we get to the end that nature would respond like a woman having birth pangs. As the time of delivery draws near, the pains become more frequent, more severe.

Interestingly, the enemy of our soul, the god of this world, has initiated a plan of his own to distract from what the Bible says concerning natural disasters. According to the god of this world, the natural disasters that are increasing are not because we are living in the last days. They are increasing because of global warming, and man is at fault. The Devil can't change what God has put in place, but he will try to explain it away. If he can get man to focus on the climate, he has successfully accomplished his goal of deception.

Society

And because lawlessness will increase, the love of many will grow cold…For as were the days of Noah, so will be the coming of the Son of Man (Matthew 24:12, 37 ESV). *The LORD saw that the wickedness of man was great in the earth, and that every intention of the thoughts of his heart was only evil continually* (Genesis 6:5 ESV). We know that God destroyed the entire old world, except Noah, his wife, his sons, and their wives. God preserved the animal world by bringing a male and female of each species into the ark.

The days of Noah were filled with violence and immorality. Genesis chapter six describes the depth of wickedness that filled the land. They were lovers of self, of money, pleasure, humanism, materialism, and hedonism, not unlike our world, and very apparent in our nation. The 1960s was the beginning of the narcissistic generation. It's all about "me" and what makes "me" feel good. Who cares about morality? I am free to do and be anything that satisfies me.

Since the 1960s, we have witnessed God removed from schools, our government, and replaced with humanistic teaching and a lifestyle with no limits. We have seen an increase in violence, sexual impurity, families destroyed, and in the last few years, more anger, hatred, and division in our nation than we have experienced since the Civil War.

Dave Reagan describes the present generation as a narcissist self-centered culture in this way.

- Their religion: Humanism. Everything revolves around the Self.
- Their God: Money Materialism.
- Their lifestyle: Hedonism Pleasure.
- Their payoff: Nihilism, *the rejection of all religious and moral principles, in the belief that life is meaningless.* A total rejection of social mores, belief that nothing is worthwhile, pointless, belief in the destruction of authority, despair.

Spiritual Nature

There is an epidemic of apostasy, false religions, and the church becoming more like the world. *Let no man deceive you by any means: for that day shall not come, except there come a falling away first, and that man of sin be revealed, the son of perdition* (2 Thessalonians 2:3).

95

The Church originally was the "called out" ones. That is called out from the world, separated from the world system, and called to have a relationship with the Creator of the universe. There was a time when the church's main concern was presenting the gospel, seeing people transformed by the power of the Holy Spirit. People's lives changed; they became a new creation, the old was gone their past was forgiven, and they took on a whole new life. They took the Bible seriously and lived by the commandments God gave them.

Jesus went on to say: Many false prophets shall rise and deceive many. We are living in a world that has an abundance of false prophets. From the New Age movement to an influx of Eastern religions, the rise of humanism, and the compromising of the gospel, people are flocking to embrace the prosperity gospel and feel-good religions.

Today, no one cares what you worship as long as you embrace what the state deems sacred. But don't dare speak against the religion of the state. The religion of the state is socialism; they embrace anything society deems moral and rejects what the Bible calls moral. It is interesting the state screams separation of church and state, yet screams if the god of the state is not first in all things. If we do not fall in step with society, we are declared intolerant, and a hater. We are living in a world where the church has surrendered its basic function, to present Christ as the only way of salvation. Much of the church has surrendered to pressure and now presents a social gospel. This is what the Bible calls, *having a form of Godliness, but denying the power thereof: from such turn away* (2 Timothy 3:5).

The function of the church seems to have been replaced by a feel-good plan that if I busy myself with doing, helping, making our society better that will satisfy God. Just don't make anyone feel uncomfortable, then perhaps they will see a need to be converted and become a Christian.

As the church, we have become shallow in trying to become seeker-friendly; as such, we have become message unfriendly. Has the church compromised the grace of God to the point that grace has no value? Dietrich Bonhoeffer, in his book, *The Cost of Discipleship,* points out that God's grace is not to be taken lightly.

> "Such grace is costly … It is costly because it cost a
> man his life, and it is grace because it gives a man the
> only true life. It is costly because it condemns sin,
> and is grace because it justifies the sinner. Above all,
> it is costly because it cost God the life of his Son: "ye
> were bought at a price," and what has cost God much
> cannot be cheap for us. Above all, it is grace because
> God did not reckon his Son too dear a price to pay for
> our life, but delivered him up for us. Costly grace is
> the Incarnation of God."[30]

The Church of Laodicea as described in Revelation 3:14-21 says the Church will grow apathetic. We see the Church today, which thinks it is wealthy with its big church buildings and big budgets, but spiritually is falling apart.

Janice, a lady in our Sunday School class, commented on the state of the church:

> "The teaching that disturbs me defines the mission
> more in line with social justice and serving the needy
> rather than spreading the message of salvation from
> sin and making disciples. I think Franklin Graham,
> with *His Samaritan's Purse* ministry, is a good example
> of meeting needs while proclaiming a strong message
> of a Savior for sinners."

World Politics

Are we living in the day of the revival of the former Roman Empire? This topic is often in the news today, so after doing some research, I found a thumbnail sketch. This article has more information if you go to their website: https://www.ucg.org/bible-study…/the-eu-a-seventh-roman-revival-in-the-making

"In 1957, six Western European nations – West Germany, France, Italy, the Netherlands, Luxembourg, and Belgium – came together to create the European Economic Community through the Treaty of Rome. These groundbreaking steps toward European unification were taken in the ancient capital city of the Roman Empire and home to one of the world's oldest and major religions."

Paul Henri Spaak, former secretary-general of NATO, later remarked on that signing in a BBC documentary: "We felt like Romans on that day…we were consciously recreating the Roman Empire once more."

"The European Union is currently a union of 25 European countries that increasingly resembles the Holy Roman Empire."

Along with the rise of the Roman Empire, there is the call for globalism, a one-world government. I was shocked to learn who was behind the call for globalism. Let me share some comments that political and influential people are saying, as Jan Markell of *Olive Tree Ministries* reported.

Walter Cronkite: In an address to the news media stated, "We Americans will have to yield up some of our sovereignty. It would take a lot of courage, a lot of faith in the new order. A system of world order, preferably a system of world governments, is mandatory. The proud nation someday will see the light and for the common good and their survival yield up their precious sovereignty."

George H.W. Bush: January 10, 1991. "We have before us the opportunity to forge for ourselves and future generations a new world order, a world where the rule of law, not the law of the jungle, governs the conduct of nations. When we are successful, and we will be, we have a real chance at this New World Order, an order in which a credible United Nations can use its peacekeeping role to fulfill the promise and vision of the United Nation's founder."

Gorbachev stated: "The threat of environmental crisis will be the key that will unlock the New World Order."

The question comes, what is needed for the globalists to initiate their plan? The globalists say the following is needed for the world to be ready to receive a one-world government.

- socialized medicine
- gun control
- big government
- higher taxes
- population reduction
- immigration
- cheap labor
- open borders
- environmentalism
- increase the debt
- international crisis
- welfare
- class warfare
- no religion except a single pagan religion

As we look over this list, it is obvious that the globalists are well on their way to achieving their desired objectives. It is also evident that we are living in the end times, as we witness the system described in the book of Revelation being promoted by world leaders.

Technology Will Increase

The book of Daniel speaks to the times we are living in right now, referencing the resurrection of the dead, the Great Tribulation, and that knowledge will increase.

> *And at that time shall Michael stand up, the great prince which standeth for the children of thy people: and there shall be a time of trouble, such as never was since there was a nation even to that same time: and at that time thy people shall be delivered, every one that shall be found written in the book. And many of them that sleep in the dust of the earth shall awake, some to everlasting life, and some to shame and everlasting contempt. And they that be wise shall shine as the brightness of the firmament; and they that turn many to righteousness as the stars forever and ever. But thou, O Daniel, shut up the words, and seal the book, even to the time of the end: many shall run to and fro, and knowledge shall be increased (Daniel 12:1-4).*

Technology is increasing exponentially; new technology is developing so fast we can't keep up with it. With satellites, the government can pinpoint any spot of planted earth and know what is happening there. There was a time when we wondered how the government would know who had the mark to buy or sell. It is no longer a question. Technology is a wonderful tool that can be used for good, and it can also be used for evil and control as we have seen in the past few years. Even today, there is a concern that our homes are not free from the intrusion of the new technology, note the new devices that are designed to spy on us in the privacy of our homes.

The prophet Daniel had no idea of what he saw concerning the end times. Therefore the angel spoke to Daniel that he was not to understand because this vision was reserved for the end time.

> *And I heard, but I understood not: then said I, O my Lord, what shall be the end of these things? And he said, Go thy way, Daniel: for the words are closed up and sealed till the time of the end* (Daniel 12:8-9).

When I was a child, I could never have conceived that technology would reach where it is today. How could people in the USA see what was happening in Europe, or Africa, at the same time it was happening? That very ability is available today. A clear sign of what the Bible says about the last days is here. This technology will make it possible for the antichrist to rule the world from a single location. People will buy into the demands because they are accustomed to government and technology controlling their lives.

Israel: Return to Their Homeland

Jesus talks of the Great Tribulation that is to come and ends with the parable of the fig tree. He said when you see the fig tree begin to bud you know that summer is near. The fig tree represents the nation of Israel. Jesus explained to His disciples that the temple would be destroyed and the Jews would be driven from their homeland and scattered all over the world until the time of the Gentiles is fulfilled. The temple was destroyed, and the Jews were driven out of Jerusalem, and Israel. Jesus said that when the Jews returned to their native homeland, you know that the end is near.

> *And they shall fall by the edge of the sword, and shall be led away captive into all nations: and Jerusalem shall be trodden down of the Gentiles, until the times of the Gentiles be fulfilled* (Luke 21:24).

As Gentiles, it would behoove us to pay attention to the signs of the times. The Jews were forbidden to return to Israel after being scattered in 70 A.D. From that time until 1917, they lived as strangers in foreign lands around the world. In 1917, the British took control of Palestine, after the defeat of Germany and Turkey in World War I.

At that time, the British gave the Jews permission to return to their homeland – under the Balfour Declaration, November 2, 1917. Within the document, there is a letter from British Foreign Secretary Arthur James Balfour to Lord Rothschild. That document made public the British support of a Jewish homeland in Palestine. For the first time since 70 A.D., the Jews were allowed to return to their homeland. 1917 was a Jubilee year, very significant to the Jewish people. For that is the year that all land was returned to its original owner, and all debts were canceled.

The Year of Jubilee

*You shall count seven weeks of years, seven times seven years, so that the time of the seven weeks of years shall give you forty-nine years. Then you shall sound the loud trumpet on the tenth day of the seventh month. On the Day of Atonement you shall sound the trumpet throughout all your land. And you shall consecrate the fiftieth year, and proclaim liberty throughout the land to all its inhabitants. It shall be a jubilee for you, when each of you shall return to his property and each of you shall return to his clan. That fiftieth year shall be a jubilee for you; in it you shall neither sow nor reap what grows of itself nor gather the grapes from the undressed vines. For it is a jubilee. It shall be holy to you. You may eat the produce of the field. In this year of jubilee each of you shall return to his property. …
You will dwell in the land securely*
(Leviticus 25:8-13, 18 ESV).

It is interesting to note that 1917 was a Jubilee year, and for the first time in about nineteen hundred years, the Jews were allowed to return to their homeland. In 1948, the United Nations agreed to give the land of Israel to the Jews. The Jews declared that the land should be called the state of Israel. The next Jubilee was 1967, it was at that time all of the Arab nations endeavored to drive the Jews into the sea. In six days, the Jews had destroyed all of the armies that came against them, thus the Six-Day War. With the defeat of the Arabs, for the first time since 70 A.D., the Jews walked into the city of Jerusalem. God has a way of keeping His promises.

Fast forward fifty years to another Jubilee. In 2017, President Donald J. Trump declared Jerusalem to be the capital of Israel. The land has been returned to the Jewish people. However, there will be wars until Jesus returns to defeat the enemy and give the Jews rest. In the meantime, we, Gentiles, need to pay attention because our time, according to what Jesus said, "is fulfilled." Jesus could call us home in the rapture at any moment. Look up, for our redemption draws near.

Ron Rhodes in a message of the end times had something interesting to say about Tim La Haye's comment concerning the miracle of Israel's return.

> "No nation in the history of the world has been able to maintain its national identity after being uprooted from its home of origin more than 300 years to at best 500 years, except Israel – the Jews. Their regathering from the four corners of the earth is intensely a miracle, and that miracle has happened in our lifetime."

While researching the Year of Jubilee, I came across a prophecy by Rabbi Judah Ben Samuel that he gave in 1217 A.D. It speaks to where we are in the end times.

The Prophecy of Jubilees by Rabbi Judah Ben Samuel. Ludwig Schneider of *Israel Today* magazine has translated Judah Ben Samuel (1140-1217) work into English. "...According to this article, Rabbi Judah Ben Samuel was a top Talmudic scholar in Germany. Just before he died in the year 1217, he prophesied that the Ottoman Turks would rule over the holy city of Jerusalem for eight jubilees. That is 400 years (8 x 50). The Ottoman Turks did take control of Jerusalem 300 years after the Rabbi's death in 1517 and as according to the prophecy, the Ottoman Turks then lost Jerusalem 400 years later in 1917. It was during WWI that British General Edmund Allenby walked into Jerusalem on Hanukkah without firing a shot in 1917. The timing of this with the holiday and the ease at which it occurred indeed make this moment of history extremely significant. The Rabbi then went on to say that after the eight jubilees, the ninth jubilee would have Jerusalem being a no-man's-land, which it was from 1917 to 1967 until the Six-Day-War. The Rabbi's prophecy then stated that in the tenth Jubilee that Jerusalem would be controlled by Israel and then the Messianic end times would begin. That would then bring the time to 2017." Very interesting. Keep in mind that Ludwig Schneider researched this before 2017.[31]

Zechariah 12:3 says, *And in that day will I make Jerusalem a burdensome stone for all people: all that burden themselves with it shall be cut in pieces, though all the people of the earth be gathered together against it.* The entire world seems to be against Israel; it has to be Satan because how can anyone hate one tiny country, and want to destroy everything about it. Our generation is the first generation to witness the rebirth of the land of Israel since the Temple was destroyed in 70 A.D. The return of Israel to their homeland is a major sign that we are living in the last days.

18

Do Not Be Deceived

When we consider that we are living in the last days, the question comes, what are the last days, and how do they affect me? For my whole life, I have thought about the end of the world and what the Bible calls "the last days." I was about ten years old the first time I heard about the world ending. I don't remember all of the details; what I do remember is I was plenty frightened. We were told that the world was going to end on a certain day, the night before I wondered about what we were told, and if I would ever see my parents and family again. The next day I woke to the world the same as it was with no change. Since that time, there have been many such predictions with the same results.

Lest you think religious people are the only ones making such claims, I have seen on the news that if we, as a nation, don't clean up our planet, we only have 12 years before the world will be destroyed. Another man showing the world globe declared that if we don't pay attention to the environment, the world will be destroyed by fire, he then set the globe on fire to emphasize his point. Are we to take these claims seriously, and if so, how are we to respond? I do not mean to make light of their claims for I believe they are fully convinced of what they are espousing but also just as convinced they are wrong.

I believe what the Bible says, and that God is totally in control of the whole situation. Peter, in speaking of the end times, said, *The heavens shall pass away with a great noise, and the elements shall melt with fervent heat, the earth also and the works that are therein shall be burned up* (2 Peter 3:10). Yes, the world will be changed as we know it, but it will be at God's command, in God's timing.

Peter went on to say that in the last days, there would be scoffers. We are seeing people scoffing at the idea of God having anything to do with the world condition, the environment, or the rapture of believers. In other words, man is responsible for the problems in the world, and the environment. It is up to man to fix his problems. As Christians, we may lose patience and wonder where is God in all of this? Again Peter says to the Christian, don't lose heart for *the Lord is not slack concerning His promises* (2 Peter 3:9).

We can trust what God said in His Word because what the prophets have prophesied in the past has come to pass 100% of the time. Take, for example, the prophecies concerning the birth, ministry, death, and resurrection of Christ. I checked out over 50 prophecies concerning Christ, and every one of them came true just as predicted. Dr. David Jeremiah in his book, *Is This The End?*, speaking about the second coming, points out, "For every prophecy in the Bible about the birth of Christ – His first coming – there are eight about His second coming"[32]

The Bible is very specific concerning prophecies. All prophecies recorded in the Bible regarding the past have come true just as predicted. We, therefore, can be sure that the prophecies concerning the second coming and end times will happen just as the Bible declares.

The events leading up to the second coming of Christ, according to scripture, include the rapture of the church, the ushering in of the one-world government, the rise of the antichrist, the Great Tribulation, the battle of Armageddon, and the millennium. I believe we are witnessing many end time signs that are coming together; it is, therefore, imperative that we pay attention to what is happening. It appears according to Bible prophecy, the next big event is the rapture of the Church. In 1 Thessalonians, the fourth chapter, the apostle Paul speaks of the blessed hope of the church and the dead in Christ. The blessed hope is the resurrection of the dead in Christ, and those who are alive being caught up to meet the Lord in the air, thus the rapture.

But I would not have you to be ignorant, brethren, concerning them which are asleep, that ye sorrow not, even as others which have no hope. For if we believe that Jesus died and rose again, even so, them also which sleep in Jesus will God bring with him. For this we say unto you by the word of the Lord, that we which are alive and remain unto the coming of the Lord shall not prevent them which are asleep. For the Lord himself shall descend from heaven with a shout, with the voice of the archangel, and with the trump of God: and the dead in Christ shall rise first: Then we which are alive and remain shall be caught up together with them in the clouds, to meet the Lord in the air: and so shall we ever be with the Lord. Wherefore comfort one another with these words (1 Thessalonians 4:13-18).

The rapture of the Church is the next event on the horizon before the return of Christ to the Mount of Olives from where He ascended after His resurrection. After Jesus met with the disciples on the mount, the Bible describing what happened is a perfect picture of the rapture, being caught up.

And when he had said these things, as they were looking on, he was lifted up, and a cloud took him out of their sight. And while they were gazing into heaven as he went, behold, two men stood by them in white robes, and said, Men of Galilee, why do you stand looking into heaven? This Jesus, who was taken up from you into heaven, will come in the same way as you saw him go into heaven (Acts 1:9-11 ESV).

All of the events that must take place before the rapture of believers have come to pass. Therefore the rapture of the Church could happen at any time. What are we to do? How are we to respond? Jesus said that His coming would be like a thief in the night; no one knows when the rapture will take place. He also said, *occupy till I come* (Luke 19:13). The message is we are to keep busy diligently working for the kingdom. Living our daily lives, expecting the trump of God to sound at any moment, to be caught up to meet the Lord in the air (1 Thessalonians 4:17). Nevertheless, as long as we are on planet Earth, we are expected to be faithful.

God has sent warning after warning to America, yet America has rejected the warnings. People don't want to hear what God has to say; they want a secular social solution. Hal Lindsey has written a book entitled, *The Late Great Planet Earth,* citing the end-time prophecy and the rapture of the church. Hollywood produced a movie called, *Left Behind,* billed as a fantasy mystery. It was based on the concept that millions suddenly vanished from the face of the earth. While Hollywood advertised it as a fantasy, the Bible declares it as a fact, one that is yet to come.

Whether the rapture takes place in our lifetime or not, we are to live as though it may. Therefore, we are to live for Christ even in the midst of struggle. The apostle Paul has given us some strong words to help us grow in times of conflict.

> *Therefore, since we have been justified by faith, we have peace with God through our Lord Jesus Christ. Through him we have also obtained access by faith into this grace in which we stand, and we rejoice in the hope of the glory of God. More than that, we rejoice in our sufferings, knowing that suffering produces endurance, and endurance produces character, and character produces hope, and hope does not put us to shame, because God's love has been poured into our hearts through the Holy Spirit who has been given to us* (Romans 5:1-5 ESV).

I have been very aware for the past several years that there has been a feeling of impending doom upon the world. Everyone seems to feel uneasy and wondering what is in the air. In 1998, David Wilkerson wrote in his book, *God's Plan In The Coming Depression*:

"Everyone senses that something is about to take place, but no one wants to face it. A lawyer friend of mine had a typical response. He said, "I know something unusual is happening and that a storm is probably coming. But I really don't want to hear about it. I just hope it blows over and everything gets back to normal as quickly as possible."[33]

That seems to be the attitude of America today. What no one seems to recognize is that we are in a cosmic war with Satan and his forces against the God of heaven. This battle has been going on since Satan was cast out of heaven, Isaiah 14 and Ezekiel 28 describe his expulsion.

The question comes, what is the hope of America, and in particular, the Christian? The only hope for America is turning away from sin and returning to the God that has so richly blessed us. 1 Chronicles 14:7 lays it out so clearly, yet there seems to be a resistance to God's plan, in favor of the humanist plan. In other words, if man is capable of fixing his problems by himself, we don't need God. Have we in America come to the place of Mars Hill where we embrace everything, including the unknown God (Acts 17:23)?

Americans are very spiritual in their own way, but they are not godly. They worship astrology, the environment, Mother Earth, idols of the hand and of the heart. Their rules have been written to fit their own desires. People are turning to the government to meet all of their needs, such as the social system be it health care, food stamps, and cradle to the grave care. I notice that animals are replacing God as a source of comfort. David Wilkerson said in his book, *God's Plan In The Coming Depression:*

"Israel's great sin is still the great sin of God's people today: a lack of respect for the presence of the Lord in their personal lives! The people lightly esteemed God's holy presence in their midst. They didn't have a craving in their hearts for communion with him. They wanted his provisions, his protection, his salvation – but not his presence!"[34]

We hear our leaders say "God Bless America", but you don't hear them say, "America, repent of your sins." The only hope for the Christian and the church is to be deeply rooted in the Word of God and stand on the solid rock, Christ Jesus.

19

How Are We To Respond?

The fact that we are living in the last days is clear, as the whole world is in turmoil and chaos. The signs are evident to anyone looking if they will compare the events to Bible prophecy. All elements are falling into place that the Bible describes as necessary for the last great battle to take place. Jesus spoke of them in Matthew 24, Mark 13, and Luke 21. However, if one wants to bury their head in the sand, there is only one solution – destruction and death.

Where does the Christian stand in this world of confusion and chaos? Jesus said, *Lift up your heads; for your redemption draweth nigh* (Luke 21:28). For the Christian, our hope is in Jesus Christ and the written Word of God – the Bible. Jesus said, *Jerusalem shall be trodden down of the Gentiles, until the times of the Gentiles be fulfilled* (Luke 21:24). With the Jews returning to their homeland and Jerusalem designated as the capital of Israel, the time of the Gentiles must be coming to a close. It would, therefore, behoove us to lift up our heads and look for the Lord to call His church home to be with Him – hence the rapture.

What is the rapture of the church? The Bible describes it as being caught up, the apostle Paul writes of this in 1 Corinthians and 1 Thessalonians.

> *Behold, I show you a mystery; We shall not all sleep, but we shall all be changed, In a moment, in the twinkling of an eye, at the last trump: for the trumpet shall sound, and the dead shall be raised incorruptible, and we shall be changed* (1 Corinthians 15:51-52).

> *But I would not have you to be ignorant, brethren, concerning them which are asleep, that ye sorrow not,*

even as others which have no hope. For if we believe that Jesus died and rose again, even so them also which sleep in Jesus will God bring with him. For this we say unto you by the word of the Lord, that we which are alive and remain unto the coming of the Lord shall not prevent them which are asleep. For the Lord himself shall descend from heaven with a shout, with the voice of the archangel, and with the trump of God: and the dead in Christ shall rise first: Then we which are alive and remain shall be caught up together with them in the clouds, to meet the Lord in the air: and so shall we ever be with the Lord. Wherefore comfort one another with these words (1 Thessalonians 4:13-18).

The rapture of the church is the last great event before Jesus returns to defeat the Devil's army and set up His earthly kingdom. As we race toward that event, how are we to live? Jesus said that His coming would be suddenly and without warning. Therefore we are to be living with the expectation that He could return at any moment. Only those who are looking for His return will be caught up to meet the Lord in the air. All others will be left on the earth to face the Great Tribulation. But the Christian has a hope that is both steadfast and sure for we are anchored to the solid rock, Christ Jesus, and the Bible (Hebrews 6:19).

For the Christian and those who are looking for the soon coming of Jesus in the clouds, what is our hope and where is our faith placed? It is evident that the world is seeking more wealth, newer homes, better and bigger toys, everything new and exciting to satisfy the physical and make life more enjoyable and fun. The whole focus is for this life – then what? The Bible says, *For what will it profit a man if he gains the whole world and forfeits his soul? Or what shall a man give in return for his soul* (Matthew 16:26 ESV)?

The stakes are high. We are dealing with eternity. Do you have doubts and are unsure that if Jesus should call today that you would be ready to meet Him? I assure you that God loves you and has provided a way for you to escape the coming judgment on planet Earth. Jesus said, *For God so loved the world, that He gave His only begotten Son, that whosoever believeth in Him should not perish, but have everlasting life* (John 3:16). The gift is free to everyone, but like any gift, it must be accepted to be of any value. Not receiving the gift will in no way diminish the value of the gift, and the gift will be of no value to anyone who rejects it.

To receive the gift of salvation, one must:

Acknowledge: That we are Sinners in Need of a Savior.

The Bible says, *for all have sinned* (Romans 3:23). The Bible also says, *For the wages of sin is death; but the gift of God is eternal life through Jesus Christ our Lord* (Romans 6:23). Wages are what we receive for the work we have done. Paul is saying we will receive the wage we worked for; if our life has been a life of sin, the wage we receive is death. Death is separation from God and eternity in hell with the god of this world, Satan. However, if we receive the gift that God has provided, we will have life eternal in heaven with Jesus.

Believe: On the Lord Jesus Christ

Believe on the Lord Jesus, and you will be saved (Acts 16:31). It is not enough to just believe that Jesus was a historical figure, or that He was a good man. The New Age teaching is Jesus was someone to show us how to live, but He was not God, and we don't need to make Him the Lord of our lives. Contrary to such teaching, some very solid ways must be accepted to qualify as believing on the Lord Jesus Christ for salvation. Jesus made some strong statements about what is needed to be saved. Jesus said, *I am the way, the truth, and the life: No one cometh unto the Father, but by me* (John 14:6). Jesus said there are not many ways to God. He emphatically stated that He was the only way. Jesus told Nicodemus, *Truly, truly, I say to you, unless one is born again, he cannot see the kingdom of God* (John 3:3 ESV).

To be born again is to have a change take place in one's life; our citizenship is transferred from this world to heaven. Paul says, *Therefore if any man be in Christ, he is a new creature: old things are passed away; behold, all things become new* (2 Corinthians 5:17). Believing in the Lord Jesus Christ is a life-changing experience, and if there is no change, we may question whether there has been an acceptable belief in Jesus.

Confess: You have received Jesus as your Lord and Savior

The Bible says, *If you confess with your mouth that Jesus is Lord and believe in your heart that God raised him from the dead, you will be saved. For with the heart one believes and is justified, and with the mouth one confesses and is saved* (Romans 10:9-10 ESV). If what we are saying doesn't agree with how we live, how we live out-weighs what we say. For us to confess that we have received Christ as our savior will make a dramatic difference in how we live. People will ask, "What happened to you?" Some will say, "You are different, what has happened?" Then we confess that we have made Jesus the Lord of our life. I have heard different stories of people that received Christ, and while their stories differ, they all expressed a transformation, and others noticed a change.

With our faith in Christ and our trust in the Bible, we can live a life of peace amid the turmoil. Let us lift our heads for our redemption draws near. We are living in this world, but we are not of this world. Having been born anew into the body of Christ, our citizenship has been transferred from this world to heaven. As Paul stated, *We are ambassadors for Christ* (2 Corinthians 5:20). We love those in the world and live at peace with the world as much as possible. But, not letting the world squeeze us into their mold causing the Christian to abandon their Christian principles to fit into what the world declares acceptable.

How does one live at peace with this world without compromising our principles? To live without compromise is a huge challenge. I believe this is a challenge that everyone must answer for themselves by placing their trust in God and the Bible to direct them in the way they should respond. We also have the Holy Spirit living within us to be our comforter, guide, teacher, and helper (John 15:26, 16:13).

The world situation is not a surprise to God. He is in control of the whole thing. As we learn from the scripture, God is working everything after the *counsel of his own will* (Ephesians 1:11). We are to take courage and stand firm in the face of impending opposition. God has always had a people who did not bow to Baal, the god of this world. God has stood by those who trust in Him even when it looked like they were being overrun by the enemy. When bad things happen, when it looks like the enemy is winning, God has a better plan. The Bible is full of situations where it looked like the enemy was winning, but God turned the tide and brought victory.

Not everything that we encounter will be pleasant; however, if we keep our focus on Jesus and the Bible, we will not be defeated. Romans 8:28 says, *And we know that all things work together for good to them that love God, to them who are the called according to his purpose.* Paul never said that all things would be good, but all things would work together for good. Hebrews, the eleventh chapter, is the *Roll Call of the Heroes of Faith.* Naming heroes of the past that suffered for their faith, some were delivered, and some were not. I am not suggesting that we will be martyred for our faith, but I believe if we stand strong and do not compromise, we may very likely be ill-treated for our stand.

It is not a stretch to think that persecution will come to America when we see how Christians are being persecuted in other lands around the world. Some have been killed for their faith, and others are driven from their homeland. The hope of the Christian is found in the Bible for Jesus said, *I will never leave thee, nor forsake thee* (Hebrews 13:5). No matter what comes our way, Jesus promised never to leave us. He may not deliver us out of the storm, but He will be with us in the storm.

We can take courage in what the Bible says, *Jesus Christ the same yesterday, and today, and forever* (Hebrews 13:8). Jesus and God's Word have not changed and will not change. The law God gave to Moses on the mountain is just as valid today as it was the day it was delivered. The hymn writer says it well.

> My hope is built on nothing less than Jesus' blood and righteousness.
> I dare not trust the sweetest frame, But wholly lean on Jesus' name.
> When darkness seems to hide His face, I rest on His unchanging grace.
> In every high and stormy gale, My anchor holds within the veil.
> His oath, His covenant, His blood support me in the whelming flood.
> When all around my soul gives way, He then is all my hope and stay.
> When He shall come with trumpet sound, oh, may I then in Him be found!
> Dressed in His righteousness alone, faultless to stand before the throne!
> On Christ, the solid rock, I stand: all other ground is sinking sand,
> All other ground is sinking sand.

About the Author

Glen O. Suiter entered the world on a hot summer day in August, 1935 in Collbran, Colorado. He was the seventh of ten children. Arriving in the middle of the Great Depression, he entered a world where making a living was very difficult. His family moved out to Oregon – the Promised Land – where his father heard there was work and plenty of opportunity.

The Suiter home was centered on God and prayer was a vital part of their family life. At the age of eight, Glen went out to the barn to be alone with God and pray. That morning he asked Jesus to come into his heart. Since then, God has been Glen's constant companion through every challenge and victory.

Due to some traumatic experiences at school in his early years, Glen gave up on learning. When he entered high school, skipping classes became the norm rather than the exception. In the spring of 1952, Glen quit school.

In October 1952, Glen was inducted into the Air Force and served four years. After his separation from the service, Glen knew it was time to give himself wholly to God and prepare for the ministry. One night in Myrtle Creek, Oregon, God met him at the altar and Glen's life was back on track.

Virginia, the best-looking girl in church, became his wife in August 1957. About a month after their wedding, Virginia's parents took a church in southern Oregon and Glen and his wife joined them there. Glen and Virginia had three children, two girls and a boy.

Up and down the West Coast from California to Alaska, Glen's employment included serving the Lord in various churches as pastor, youth pastor, and worship leader. His secular jobs included construction work, logging work, and tour bus driver.

After the age of 60, Glen reentered college with the desire to complete his degree. Spring semester of 2002, the National Dean's List honored him as one of America's outstanding college students. It was a testimony to the blessing of God and a confirmation he wasn't as dumb as his third grade teacher made him out to be.

While pastoring in Palmer, Alaska in July 2004, after 46 years of marriage, his wife Virginia died of heart failure. Glen's life was a blur as he moved ahead without her.

Some time passed and Glen began to think about marriage. God had a wife picked out for Glen. He was reintroduced to a long-time friend, Donna, who lived in Salem, Oregon. Three months later, they were married in Alaska. Donna has been a constant help and support to Glen's life and ministry.

Currently, Glen and Donna live in Spokane, Washington. Glen teaches a weekly Sunday School class called "Practical Christian Living." His passion is to share the truth of God's Word and help others navigate the storms of life. Glen is also the author of "This Is My Story: Growing in Grace."

Bibliography

Bonhoeffer, Dietrich. *The Cost of Discipleship.* A Touchstone Book Published by Simon & Schuster, first published 1937

Borg, Marcus J. *Reading the Bible Again for the First Time.* Harper San Francisco, A division of Harper Collins Publishers, 2001

Chambers, Oswald. *My Utmost for His Highest.* Discovery House Publishers, 1992

Charnock, Stephen. *The Existence and Attributes of God.* Reprinted by Baker Books, Baker Publishing Group, 1996

Graham, Billy. *Hope for Each Day.* Published by J. Countryman, a division of Thomas Nelson, Inc., 2002

Gurnall, William. *The Christian in Complete Armor.* Hendrickson Publishers Marketing LLC, 2010

Kupelian, David. *The Marketing of Evil.* WMD Books, 2005

Lindstedt, David. *Faith's Great Heroes.* Barbour Publishing Incorporated, 1999

Lutzer, Erwin. *Hitler's Cross.* Moody Publishers, 1995

Lutzer, Erwin. *The Serpent of Paradise.* Moody Publishers, 1996

Morey, Robert. *The Battle of the Gods.* Crown Publications, 1989

Murray, Andrew. *The Believer's Prayer Life.* Bethany House Publishers, August 1983

Packer, J.I. *Knowing God.* IVP Books, 1973

Rutz, James. *MegaShift.* Empowerment Press, 2005

Spence, Robert. *The Politically Incorrect Guide to Islam*. Regnery Publishing Inc., 2005

Thomas, Major W. Ian. *The Indwelling Life of Christ*. Multnomah Books, 2006

Wilkerson, David. *God's Plan In The Coming Depression*. Wilkerson Trust Publications, 1998

Zacharias, Ravi. *Why Jesus?* Thomas Nelson, 1973

Internet Resources

Walsch, Neale Donald. Conversations with God: An Uncommon Dialogue.

Temple Of Baal Gateway Arch Is Going Up In New York City ... https://www.silverdoctors.com/headlines/world-news/temple-of-baal-gateway-arch-nyc-new-york-city/

American Humanist Association, https://americanhumanist.org

Manifesto II, https://americanhumanist.org/

The Supreme Court Decision, https://supreme.justia.com/cases/federal/us/449/64/

Public Schools and Introduction to Islam, https://fortressoffaith.com/how-islam-is-being-introduced-into-our-public-schools/

Kurtz, Paul who published the Manifestos in 1973, https://en.wikipedia.org/wiki/Humanist_Manifesto_II

Goddess Kali, https://www.youtube.com/watch?v=U266P7QrBds

Reagan, Dave. Lamb and Lion Ministries. https://christinprophecy.org

World politics - Markel, Jan. https://www.ucg.org/bible-study.../the-eu-a-seventh-roman-revival-in-the-making

End Notes

Chapter 2
1   Bonhoeffer, Dietrich. *The Cost of Discipleship*. Page 204
2   Gurnall, William. *The Christian in Complete Armor*. Page 121

Chapter 3
3   Gurnall, William. *The Christian in Complete Armor*. Page 131
4   Gurnall, William. *The Christian in Complete Armor*. Page 125

Chapter 5
5   Zacharias, Ravi. *Why Jesus?*. Pages 14 and 16
6   Bonhoeffer, Dietrich. *The Cost of Discipleship*. Page 30
7   Zacharias, Ravi. *Why Jesus?*. Pages 129 and 130
8   Zacharias, Ravi. *Why Jesus?*. Page 201
9   Zacharias, Ravi. *Why Jesus?*. Page 202
10 Zacharias, Ravi. *Why Jesus?*. Page 210
11 Rutz, James. *Megashift*. Page 135
12 Walsch, Neale Donald. Internet: Conversations with God: An Uncommon Dialogue. Book 1
13 Spence, Robert. *The Politically Incorrect Guide to Islam*. Page 3
14 Chambers, Oswald. *Conformed to His Image*. Page 21
15 Lutzer, Erwin. *The Serpent of Paradise*. Page 172
16 Thomas, Major W. Ian. *The Indwelling Life of Christ*. Page 168

Chapter 6
17 Walsch, Neale Donald. Internet: Conversations with God: An Uncommon Dialogue. Book 1
18 Gurnall, William. *The Christian in Complete Armor*, Volume 2. Page 55

Chapter 7

19 Packer, J.I. *Knowing God*. Page 196
20 Lindstedt, David. *Faith's Great Heroes*. Page 127
21 Lutzer, Erwin. *Hitler's Cross*. Page 149
22 Lutzer, Erwin. *The Serpent of Paradise*. Page 130

Chapter 8

23 Gurnall, William. *The Christian in Complete Armor*, Volume 2. Page 8
24 Chambers, Oswald. *My Utmost for His Highest,* July 16
25 Murray, Andrew. *The Believer's Prayer Life*. Page 24

Chapter 9

26 Graham, Billy. *Hope for Each Day*. March 9th

Chapter 10

27 Oden, Thomas C. *A Change of Heart*. Page 81

Chapter 13

28 Bonhoeffer, Dietrich. *The Cost of Discipleship*. Page 27
29 Bonhoeffer, Dietrich. *The Cost of Discipleship*. Page 30

Chapter 17

30 Bonhoeffer, Dietrich. *The Cost of Discipleship*. Page 45

Chapter 18

31 The Coming Shemitah & Jubilee Year 5774/5 – Pray4Zion
32 Jeremiah, Dr. David. *Is This The End?*. Page 241
33 Wilkerson, David. *God's Plan In The Coming Depression*. Page 104
34 Wilkerson, David. *God's Plan In The Coming Depression*. Page 113